THE BOOK OF WINDSURFING

THE BOOK OF
WINDSURFING
A Guide to Freesailing Techniques

Mike Gadd

John Boothroyd

Ann Durrell

 Van Nostrand Reinhold Ltd., Toronto
New York, Cincinnati, London, Melbourne

LIBRARY OF CONGRESS CATALOGUE NUMBER 79-57606

Canadian Cataloguing in Publication Data

Gadd, Mike
  The book of windsurfing

ISBN 0-442-29729-7 pa.

1. Windsurfing. I. Boothroyd, John, 1948–
II. Durrell, Ann, 1953–   III. Title.

GV811.63.W56B66   797.1´24   C80-094159-4

Acknowledgments
The authors and publisher wish to express their gratitude to those who have provided photographs for use in this book. For a complete list of acknowledgments, please see page 128, which for legal purposes is considered to form part of the copyright page.

Design: Brant Cowie/Artplus Ltd.
Illustrations: Krista Johnston
Cover Photograph: Steve Wilkings
Typesetting: Trigraph Inc.
Printing and Binding: Johanns Graphics Limited
Printed and bound in Canada

80 81 82 83 84 85 86 7 6 5 4 3 2 1

Published in the United States of America
by Van Nostrand Reinhold Company, New York.

757595O

To Arlene Francis Boothroyd

Contents

Mike Gadd freesailing in the Gulf of Mexico.

Foreword

In February 1980, while the Winter Olympics were in full swing at Lake Placid, the International Olympic Committee accepted in principle the scheduling of boardsailing (also called freesailing or windsurfing) as one of seven Olympic Yachting Events. To say that the rise of the sailboard to this pinnacle of yachting has been meteoric would, at best, be an understatement.

Scarcely ten years have gone by since the Windsurfer® made its debut to the yachting establishment at the "America's Tea Cup Regatta," a one-of-a-kind type of event sponsored by **One Design Yachtsman** for all boardboats and the like. In retrospect, it was quite an event since, at the same time, the Laser (a boat that has revolutionized singlehanded dinghy sailing) also made its first public appearance.

Interestingly enough, unlike many new inventions in traditional activities, the Windsurfer® captured the imagination of the yachting public almost immediately and in large measure has had the support of the establishment ever since its inception, far more so, for example, than has the multihull sailboat.

One must suppose that the sailor's fascination with the sailboard comes from the pure beauty and naturalness of it. Almost as much a hang glider as it is a sailboat, the rig provides a sailboard with its fantastic performance by supporting the weight of the sailor more and more as the wind and speed increase until such time as the sailboard literally skips along the surface of the water displacing only its own weight and flying free of the normal constraints that limit the performance of conventional sailboats.

Not only has the yachting public accepted the sailboard, but also a new public that has never been on the water has seen the sailboard as a wonderfully exciting activity. Statistics in new sports are always hard to pin down, but it appears that nearly 400,000 sailboards exist today and that 200,000 will be sold in the year 1980. By yachting standards, that's an incredible number.

With this rapid growth a pile of problems have arisen, in particular those that relate to access and rights to the waterways, legal jurisdiction and insurance. Partially for these reasons and partially because of the phenomenal growth of the sport in Europe, it was only a matter of time before the International Yacht Racing Union (the international federation for the sport of yachting) decided that sailboards were yachts and that they should become part of the sailing community.

In 1978 the IYRU established a Boardsailing Committee specifically to work with the various international agencies, to try to help protect the rights of the boardsailor and to help frame international legislation guaranteeing those rights. In 1980 the IYRU granted "international status" to Windsurfer® and the Windglider®, the two largest sailboard classes and proposed the yachting part of the Olympic Games be expanded to include boardsailing as one of the events.

For a variety of reasons the sailboard has grown in popularity much more rapidly in Europe. "Why" is the subject of much speculation but perhaps the best reason is that in Europe the growth of the activity was largely created by sailing schools which offered free or inexpensive lessons to anyone buying a board. In North America, on the other hand, owners of new boards were pretty much left on their own to figure it out for themselves.

Boardsailing, contrary to its early reputation, is not difficult to learn but it sure is different! This I can say with conviction as a result of personal experience. It took me two afternoons to learn how to get around pretty comfortably under most conditions and I am 46 years old. In terms of complexity, boardsailing is roughly as difficult to learn as riding a bicycle.

While it helps to have sailed before, it's certainly not essential. The sailboard is probably the most sensitive of all sailing machines because it is sailed, trimmed and steered exclusively by balancing the boat and by being in perfect harmony with the wind and sea. In other words you can't fake it! For this reason, it is the purest form of sailing and will teach any sailor things that he never knew about the wind and about why boats move.

It is possible to teach oneself to sail a board but it helps to have someone guide you through the first steps. In the case of a beginner who has never sailed any boat at all, it almost becomes a necessity but it isn't essential that those lessons come in the form of an instructor. This book does that job nicely and I am sure that if I had had it when I first tried boardsailing, I would have cut the first phase of learning at least in half. For a beginner, it should make the difference between a successful start and pure frustration.

Where the sport will go is anyone's guess. Far from being limited to around the buoys racing, sailboards are being used in team games of buoy ball, match slalom racing, freestyle events, long-distance events and, most spectacular of all, wave jumping in the surf. One thing is certain, in time sailboarding will attract more people to the water than will have any other type of sailing. The principles that make the board so effective a performer will surely be incorporated into a far larger craft but to those of us who just love sailing, the sailboard is like a fountain of youth that will give us something to smile about as long as we can carry a board under one arm and a sail under the other.

Andy Kostanecki, Vice Chairman, Centerboard Boat and Board-sailing Committee, International Yacht Racing Union

Preface

In the years that we have been freesailing, the sport has mushroomed. More boards are on the market, more uses of the board have been found and more people, young and old, are discovering this unique sport and the lifestyle that it offers.

We felt that there was a need for a clear, concise book on freesailing (or windsurfing and boardsailing as it is also called). **The Book of Windsurfing** is intended to teach the beginner the basics and to introduce him or her to competitive freesailing, wave surfing and other exciting aspects of the sport. We hope this book will persuade you to join the world of freesailing—a world we have come to love.

There are a number of people who have helped us with the book. We would like to thank Stan Louden, a good critic and friend, Krista Johnston for her marvelous illustrations and Andy Kostanecki, who wrote the Foreword. Thanks also to Fitzwright-Sine Limited (Bare) and North Sails and a special thank you to photographers Steve Hill, Sara Lee and Steve Wilkings.

Freesailing is a sport for all ages.

The History of Freesailing

The original board, the Windsurfer.®

Like many successful sports that emerged in the 1960s and 1970s, freesailing originated in California. James Drake, a sailor, and Hoyle Schweitzer, a surfing enthusiast, invented the first freesail craft, a surfboard and wishbone boom/sail combination. After several prototypes were built, the new invention was patented and marketed beginning in 1969 by Hoyle Schweitzer. From a home-based operation at Pacific Palisades, Hoyle and his wife, Diane, built up a large international market. By 1979 their company, Windsurfer International Incorporated, was able to produce 700 boats a week.

Freesailing caught on quickly in Europe. In 1973 a Dutch textile company, Ten Cate, began marketing the Windsurfer® product. The growing market was attractive to others and today in Europe there are over 300,000 boards and approximately 100 different brands. The sport is also enjoying great success in other areas of the world: Japan, Australia and South Africa to name a few.

The success of the freesail craft can be attributed to low cost, small size and durability. However, one very important factor in its success was timeliness. Freesailing arrived at a time when men and women were pursuing physical fitness and were moving away from motor-powered sports. Admittedly, at first, the general public was skeptical. Many people did not take the new sport seriously and dismissed it as a fad.

In the United States freesailing spread from California to Hawaii, where Kailua Beach is now one of the best freesailing areas in the world. It next became popular in Florida and New England, the home of a number of top international freesailors. Although the sport is most popular on the coasts, it is gradually spreading into the central states.

In Canada freesailing began in a small community in the Kawartha Lakes region of Ontario. Well-known Canadian free-sailing areas include Collingwood, Ontario; Mont Tremblant, Quebec; and Whistler, British Columbia.

Naturally the development of the freesail craft and the sport has not stopped with one product. Freesailing pioneers are branching out into new areas. The incredible diversity of the boats and the people who pursue the sport have resulted in many new developments. For example, hulls with footstraps have made wave jumping possible and harnesses attaching the sailor to the boom have made long-distance trips a reality rather than a dream.

Competitions are also changing. Olympic triangle racing used to be considered the ultimate racing test. A strong international association of Olympic triangle racers proves that it is still a worthwhile competition; however, the versatility of the craft has led to other competitive events. The freestyle competition, a new gymnastic approach to the sport, was introduced in 1975 and long-distance races were first held in 1976. Both one design class racing (where sailors compete on identical pieces of equipment) and open class racing (where sailors compete on different brands) have flourished. In fact, some freesailors believe open class races, which started in Europe, will dominate the race scene in the upcoming years. Dennis Davidson, a Hawaiian sailor, thinks the sport "will go the way of surfing. There will be large open class regattas with cash prizes."

Perhaps the most exciting new development has been the recent acceptance of the Windsurfer® and Windglider® as class boats by the International Yacht Racing Union. This has paved the way for the boat's acceptance as a demonstrator class in the 1984 Olympics. Basically this means that the sport will be given a trial run in 1984 to see if it achieves a certain level of competition. Participants will be able to win medals, and after this demonstration year the sport should be given full Olympic status. Freesailors have mixed feelings about this particular development. Some feel that the level of competition will increase to the point where the present easy-going atmosphere surrounding regattas will suffer. Others feel that Olympic status will help bring the sport to the attention of a larger segment of the population.

The history of freesailing is still new. We invite you to become a part of it.

Meeting new friends at a regatta.

CHAPTER 1
Knowing the Wind

What do you know about the wind? Can you point out its direction and estimate its strength? If you can answer yes to this question, you are well on your way to a successful first attempt at freesailing. If you are uncertain, no matter; it is easy to learn about the wind.

Let us assume that you are on the shore of a lake or ocean, gazing out over the water and contemplating your first try at freesailing. You have been asked to point out the direction of the wind. Here are some clues that will help you.

The first and most obvious clue is the waves that the wind is creating. Waves travel parallel to the wind direction and will give you a good idea of where the wind is coming from. If there are any birds on the beach, note the direction they face. A bird will always face directly into the wind to keep its feathers from ruffling and to prepare it for take-off. Birds take off into the wind and land facing the wind. Look for a flag in the area. It will also give you an accurate reading of the wind's direction. The most intimate knowledge of the wind comes, of course, from feeling it on your body. Try to be aware of the movement of air over your skin.

Once you have pinpointed the source of the wind, you should give some thought to its strength. Knowing the wind's strength is important to a successful learning experience for a number of reasons.

Learning to freesail is next to impossible unless the wind is light and fairly constant. Light winds do not generate much wave action and relatively calm water is essential to good balance on the boat. You will want your first attempt to be enjoyable and proper conditions are essential.

A glassy surface on the water indicates that there is no wind and any thought of sailing in such conditions should be abandoned. A freesail craft will not move without wind! If the wind is strong and the water is being whipped into large, frothy waves, again do not venture out for your first attempt. When whitecaps begin to appear with a regular frequency, the wind is approaching 15 knots and will overpower a novice sailor.

Gusty wind is a problem for the freesailor because it does not provide the constant force required for good balance on the board. Often the wind will puff hard and overpower the sailor, die out suddenly or change direction. Being able to read these shifts and gusts prepares you for the changes of sail trim that you must make to stay in control. Here again, the visual effect of the wind on the water's surface is a key. Small ripples moving more rapidly than the regular motion of the larger waves and appearing as dark patches signal surges of wind. Paying close attention to these areas of "black water" will save you from some frustrating moments and enhance your awareness of the wind.

Relatively calm water is ideal for the beginner. The wind speed should set a flag to a lazy undulation and begin to ruffle your hair.

After you have learned to freesail, you may want to be more precise in your measurement of the wind. An anemometer to measure the speed of the wind and a compass to determine its direction are useful. If you don't want to buy these instruments, a quick call to the local weather office will give you all the meteorological information that you will need to plan your sailing day.

Points of Sail

Because a freesail craft is dependent on the wind for its mobility, it is handy to refer to where you are going (your point of sail) in relation to the wind direction. Although the following manoeuvers and terms may sound complicated, with a little practice they will become second nature to you.

Sailing upwind, or toward the wind, is called **beating**. Because it is impossible to sail directly into the wind, a freesailor must approach an upwind destination by sailing a zigzag course toward it. The closest angle onto the wind that a freesail craft can point is roughly 45°, and when sailing that course, a boat is said to be sailing **close hauled**.

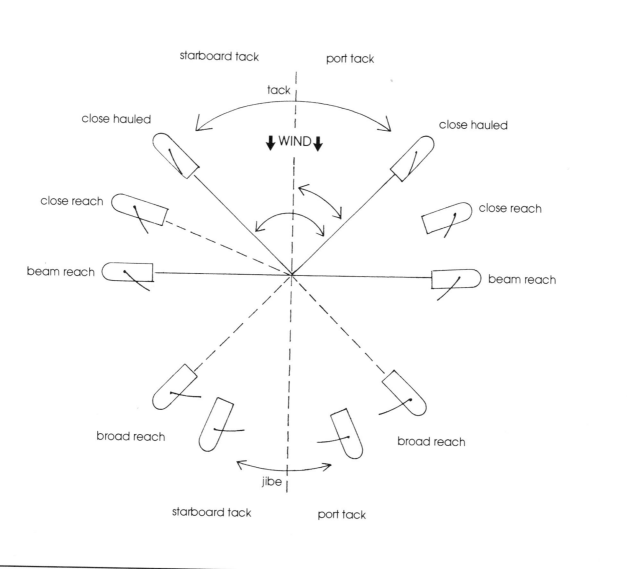

Figure 1. Points of sail

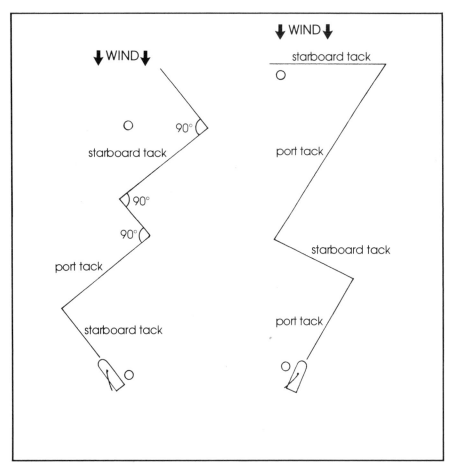

Figure 2. Beating upwind on a starboard and port tack

When sailing at any angle across the wind, a freesail craft is said to be **reaching** or **on a reach**. A course 90° to the wind is called a **beam reach**. Sailing above that course (closer to the wind) is called a **close reach**. A course below a beam reach (away from the wind) is called a **broad reach**.

Every day you go out on the water and freesail is a unique experience. The wind is such an illusive, invisible element. It's never the same. You may have gusts to contend with or swirls. Each day is different. ANDY JONES, TORONTO FREESAILOR

Preparing to to

When the wind is coming from directly behind, the craft is **on a run** or **running with (or before) the wind**.

The left side of a boat when viewed from the stern is called the **port** side, while the right side is called the **starboard** side. When the wind is filling the left side of the sail, the craft is said to be on a **port tack**. With the right side full, the craft is on a **starboard tack**. A freesail craft is always **on a tack** unless it is in the process of changing from one tack to the other. This change of tacks is called **tacking** when the boat is moving upwind or **jibing** when the boat is moving downwind.

Preparing to jibe.

Heading up refers to steering onto a course closer to the wind. When a craft points higher than 45° onto the wind, that is above being close hauled. The sail begins to flutter at the front, because it is impossible to trim it properly and still make way. The craft stalls. When the hull is pointing due upwind, it is said to be **in irons** or **head to wind**. When the sail is trimmed to neither tack and flapping loosely, it is said to be **luffing**.

Bearing off refers to steering onto a course away from the wind. A freesail craft can run before the wind on either tack and maintain the same course downwind.

Learning about the wind, feeling its power and coming to terms with it is an interesting experience. Try drawing the points of sail in the sand. Once you are familiar with them you are ready to learn how to rig and launch your freesail craft.

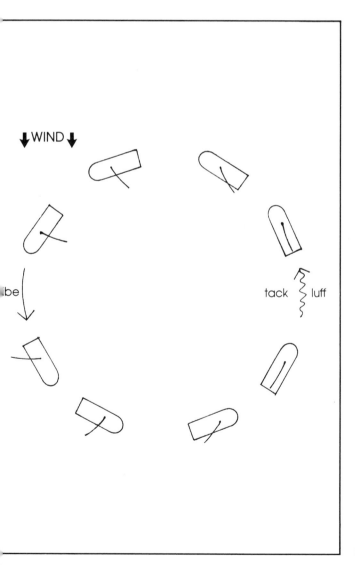

Figure 3. Sailing in a counter-clockwise circle

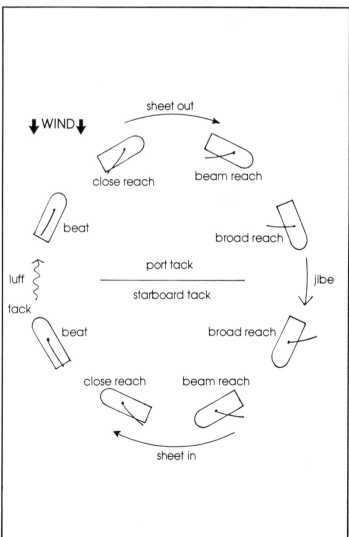

Figure 4. Sailing in a clockwise circle

CHAPTER 2
Rigging and Launching

One of the attractions of freesailing is the short length of time it takes to rig the craft. The freesail system has only three main parts: the rig, the hull and the daggerboard and skeg. You are a substitute for the wires and lines that seemingly clutter the deck of a conventional sailboat. You are also the tiller and rudder that are so obviously missing from the stern of the boat. Rigging takes a matter of minutes and launching is as easy as entering the water for a swim.

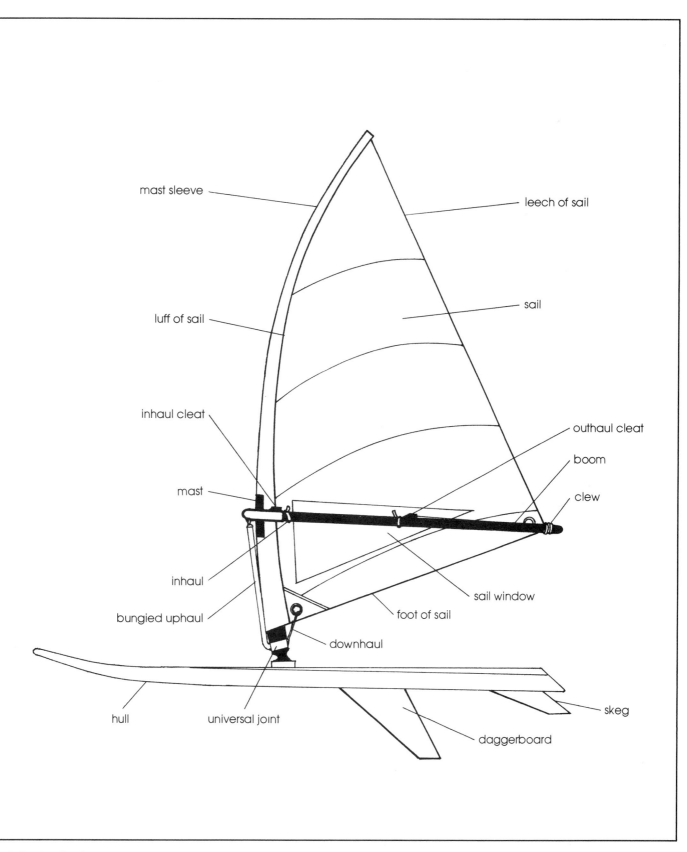

mast sleeve

leech of sail

luff of sail

sail

inhaul cleat

outhaul cleat

boom

mast

clew

inhaul

bungied uphaul

sail window

foot of sail

downhaul

hull

universal joint

skeg

daggerboard

Figure 5. Parts of a freesail craft

Parts of a Freesail Craft

Rig   This is your power source. The rig is comprised of the sail, mast and wishbone booms, which give the sail its shape and rigidity. It is attached to the hull by a device (a universal joint) that allows full rotation of the rig but does not support it in an upright position. The rig is pulled from the water to the upright position with the uphaul line.

Hull   The hull is filled with polyurethane foam and is unsinkable. It has a fitting to take the mast base, a slot amidships for the daggerboard, and fittings for a skeg or fin on the bottomside at the stern. The deck surface has a roughened texture for good traction.

Daggerboard and Skeg   The daggerboard is the larger of the two and goes through the hull like a knife just aft of the mast base. It keeps the boat from slipping sideways through the water and makes it possible to sail to windward. The size of the skeg or fin determines the ease with which the craft is steered. A small skeg gives less lateral resistance, which makes it easier to steer the boat. A large skeg gives more lateral resistance, which provides greater board stability and control at higher speeds.

Rigging

The many available freesail systems have component variations that make it difficult to describe specific rigging procedures for each type. The following general guidelines and the illustrated directions on page 27 apply to all boats and will enable you to rig your craft for maximum performance.

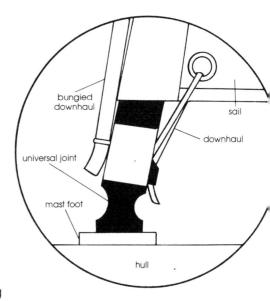

Figure 5A. Universal joint

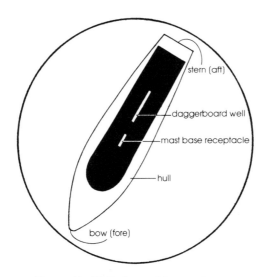

Figure 5B. Hull viewed from above

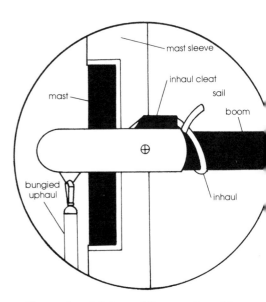

Figure 5C. Joining of the mast and boom

The sail is fixed to the mast by simply sliding the mast into the sail sleeve. The inhaul line, which attaches the booms to the mast, is tied permanently to the mast with a clove-hitch knot (see page 27). Once tightened, this knot will maintain the desired boom height. Experimentation determines the height, but the rule of thumb is: if you are short, keep the booms low in the sleeve opening. Increasing height and ability require a boom position that approaches the top of the sleeve opening.

The next step is to attach the booms, keeping in mind that the more tightly they are tied to the mast, the easier the rig is to use in all conditions. This is accomplished by placing the booms parallel to the mast and ensuring that no slack exists in the inhaul line when it is cleated to the booms. Now swing the booms square to the mast and you have the desired snug connection.

Pull the clew of the sail toward the opposite end of the booms and pass the outhaul line through the ring in the sail. Pull the sail as flat as is required by the wind conditions. In a strong wind, you will want the sail as flat as possible, so pull the clew right out to the boom end and cleat the outhaul line. In lighter winds, the outhaul can be slackened to give the sail a fuller shape.

The last attachment on the rig is the downhaul line. This line attaches the rig to the mast base and also controls the shape of the sail. Tie it snugly for light air conditions; increase the tension for stronger winds. This tension holds the airfoil shape of the sail toward the mast, countering the wind's tendency to stretch the sail out of shape.

Launching

There are various methods of launching the craft to suit the launch site and the sailor's ability. In areas where access to the water is difficult, such as along a rocky shoreline, breakwater or high wharf, or when one's boat handling abilities have yet to be developed, it is easiest to throw the rig a few yards out into the water. Follow quickly carrying the hull. Place the mast base into the hull, insert the daggerboard, hoist the rig and sail off.

A sandy beach where the water gets gradually deeper is the best site for launching a freesail craft (see page 34). Rig the sail, attach it to the hull and sling the daggerboard on your arm. Hoist the sail from the windward or downwind side of the hull (the side that faces and is nearer to the wind) and hold the mast just below the booms with your fore hand, allowing the sail to luff freely. Grasp the stern of the hull with your aft hand and walk the craft into the water. Insert the daggerboard when you are in three feet (one metre) of water, step up onto the hull, trim the sail and move off. This method requires some skill and practice, but it is the best and quickest way to get your craft onto the water.

Rigging

Assembling the Sail and Mast

The inhaul line is attached permanently to the mast with a clove-hitch knot.

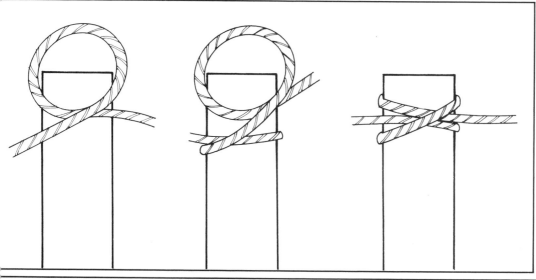

Clove-hitch knot.

Remove the sail from the sail bag, unfold and lay it on the ground. If your sail requires battens, this is the time to put them in.

Slide the mast into the sail sleeve.

If you are tall, place the inhaul line higher on the mast.

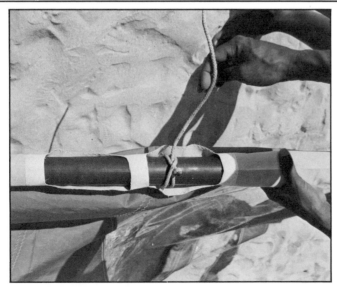

If you are short, place the inhaul line lower on the mast.

Attaching the Booms

Put the wishbone booms parallel to the mast, placing the front of the booms as close to the inhaul line as possible.

Use the inhaul line to join the mast snuggly to the booms.

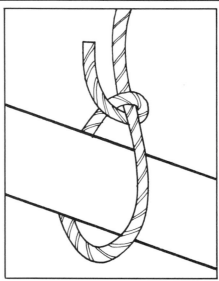

Cleat and tie off the rema ing inhaul line with a half-hitch knot.

Half-hitch knot.

Pull the clew of the sail toward the opposite end of the booms.

Pass the outhaul line through the ring in the sail and pull the sail as flat as is required by the wind conditions. Pull tighter for high winds, looser for light winds.

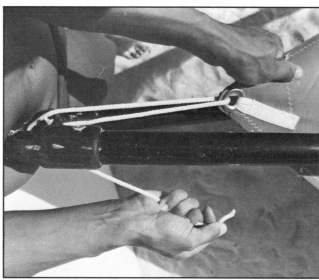

Cleat the outhaul line and tie off the excess with a half-hitch knot.

Attaching the Rig to the Board

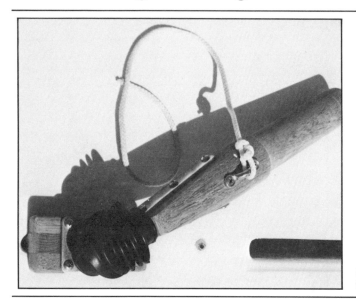

Place the universal joint into the board.

Slide the mast onto the universal joint.

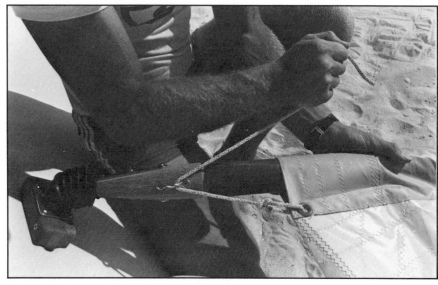

Pass the downhaul line through the ring in the sail and pull to the desired sail shape.

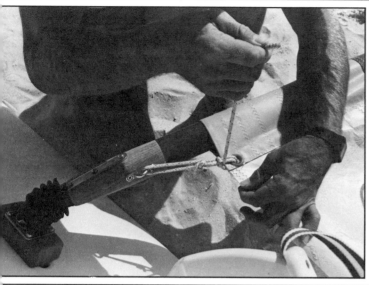

Tie the downhaul line snuggly for light wind conditions and very tightly for higher winds.

You are now rigged and ready to launch.

Launching

With the daggerboard over one arm, hoist the sail from the windward side of the hull and hold the mast just below the booms with your fore hand, letting the sail luff freely.

Place your aft hand in the daggerboard well, lift the craft and walk it into the water.

Drop the craft in approximately three feet (one metre) of water.

Place the daggerboard in the daggerboard well.

Step up onto the hull.

Follow the basic steps for getting under way in the next chapter.

Getting Under Way

To get under way, the freesailor stands on the hull straddling the mast, pulls the sail up with the uphaul line, positions the rig in front of him, grasps the boom and trims the sail onto the wind. The craft is steered by raking or leaning the sail toward the bow of the boat to bear off the wind or toward the stern to bring the boat up into the wind. How quickly you are able to learn these manoeuvers depends on several factors. By following the five basic steps outlined in this chapter and by trying to be sensitive to the response of the craft, you should have a successful first attempt with a minimum of falls. Choosing the right equipment, weather conditions and location are also important.

Equipment

A number of equipment options make learning much easier. A light rig with an aluminum rather than a wooden boom is easier to use. A wide hull gives greater stability and more buoyancy than a narrow one. It will help you maintain your balance and stay dry. Most freesail craft are sold with a standard full-sized sail, approximately sixty square feet in area. However, a smaller sail is often better for the beginner. The one you choose should match your body size and ability to the wind strength (see Diagram 1). Many freesailing schools have a full range of sails to permit instruction in a number of different weather conditions.

As your confidence grows and your skills develop, you will move on to faster hulls and larger, more powerful sails (see Chapter 5).

Dryland Exercises

The most important stage of the learning experience is what is done on land. A half hour of simulation on land equals two hours on the water. Learn to manoeuver and balance the rig with the aid of a

Jenny Ladner, the Canadian women's champion, demonstrates how to practise on dry land.

freesailing school's simulator, a machine that turns a hull 360°. Or simply stand on the hull on the ground. (Be sure to dig a hole in the sand for the skeg or remove it.) Simulate sailing on both tacks and practise the movements of bearing off and heading up.

Weather Conditions and Location

Choose the day for your first try very carefully. Look for flat water conditions and very light winds. A consistent onshore wind (blowing from the water to the land) is reliable and will not push you too far offshore before you are ready.

Be sure to wear proper clothing for the air and water temperatures (see Chapter 12). Being cold immediately puts a damper on one's enthusiasm, concentration and endurance. A wetsuit will keep you warm and deck shoes or running shoes will protect your feet if you are sailing in rocky, shallow water. A life jacket is also a necessity for the beginner.

The best place to introduce yourself to freesailing is a secluded spot away from powerboat traffic. Leave yourself lots of room to make those inevitable first mistakes and try not to be frustrated by a few falls.

The five steps for getting under way on the following pages are intended for your first try on water; however, they should be practised on land first. If an instructor is not available, have a friend read these steps to you to guide your progress.

The Five Steps for Getting Under Way

Squaring Up

Set up the craft with the sail on the downwind side. Place the daggerboard in the daggerboard well.

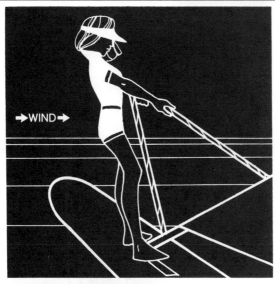

Stand on the hull with your feet on either side of the mast base, and grasp the uphaul line with both hands, squaring the hull to the mast. Begin to hoist the rig by pulling hand over hand on the uphaul, until the mast is upright enough for the clew of the booms to swing freely. Allow the sail to luff. The craft will drift slowly with the wind. Hold the rig in front of you. The mast should be perpendicular to the boat. This will keep the hull square to the wind.

Take hold of the rig by the mast with fairly straight arms, back and legs, and find a comfortable point of balance.

Now try turning the hull by leaning the sail forward toward the bow of the boat.

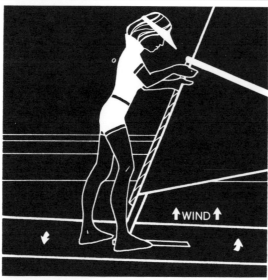

Now try turning the hull by leaning the sail aft toward the stern of the boat.

The next step is to turn the hull full circle. Keep the sail luffing and the wind at your back. Stand with your feet close to the mast base and walk the hull around. Once the rotation is complete, stop the boat by holding the rig in a neutral central position and lean the sail toward the opposite end of the boat, initiating a turn in the opposite direction. Bringing the hull full circle, stopping it again in the square position with the rig leaning toward the bow, **jibes** the boat around—the bow passes under the sail. Leaning the rig toward the stern **tacks** the boat around—the stern passes under the sail. You are now able to position the craft in the square position and ready to get under way.

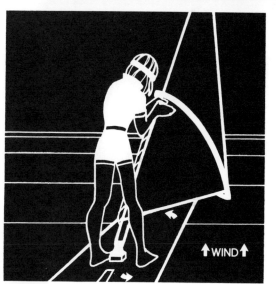

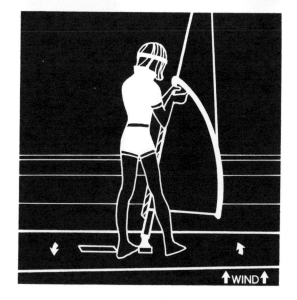

2. Sighting a Heading

Look around the horizon for a buoy on the water or a building on land to use as a potential heading. By selecting a number of points of reference around you, you are better prepared to keep your bearings. Check the water behind you for gusts and get comfortable without having to look at the hull or sail. Remember, you have to be able to see where you are going!

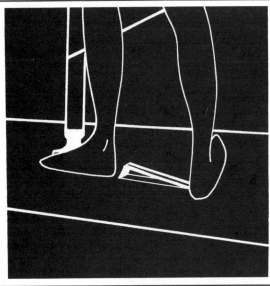

With the fore hand on the mast, move your feet so they straddle the daggerboard, keeping the fore foot close to the mast base and pointing toward the bow.

Pull the sail across in front of you by rotating your hips and shoulders toward the bow. You should now be sighting your chosen heading. Lean the sail fore or aft to maintain that heading and keep the boat square.

. Grasping the Boom

Place your aft hand on the boom almost three feet (one metre) back from the mast. Keep the sail luffing and the hull square.

Quickly move your fore hand from the mast to a position one foot (30 centimetres) back from the mast, again keeping the boat square and the sail luffing.

4. Trimming the Sail

→WIND→

Now simultaneously push the mast toward the bow of the boat with the fore hand as you pull in with the aft hand to bring the sail across the wind and more in line with the hull. This is a combined move of raking the sail forward and sheeting in. Try to keep the pull balanced on both arms.

5. Getting Under Way

↑WIND↑

Lean back against the increasing pull of the sail by bending your aft leg and push the hull forward with your straight fore leg. Both arms should be almost fully extended for proper balance. Repeat the five steps a number of times before sailing too far. Turn the boat around and do it again on the opposite tack until you are familiar and comfortable with getting under way on both tacks.

Solving Problems

If problems, such as a gust hitting the sail, are experienced at any stage, simply release the boom with the aft hand, hold on to the boom with the fore hand and come back into the initial square position to start again. Try to avoid dropping the sail. Hoisting it a number of times from the water can be tiring. However, if you do lose control, the freesail craft will come to a halt immediately as soon as the sail is dropped and hits the water. If you fall from the hull, simply swim back to it, climb on and start again.

Should the wind die out or become too strong, sit down on the hull, remove the mast from its fitting, uncleat the outhaul line and furl the sail around the mast. Swing the booms parallel to the mast and secure them with the outhaul. Lay this package on the hull, lie on it and paddle ashore using your hands. Remember, it takes patience to learn freesailing. If you start to feel tired, don't feel embarrassed about furling the sail and paddling in.

After you have mastered the five basic steps, you are well on your way to becoming a proficient freesailor.

Diagram 1. Sail Choice for Learning Situations

Wind Strength in Knots / Sailor's Weight in Pounds	50–100	100–125	125–150	150–175	175 +
2–5	Storm	Marginal	Marginal	Full	Oversize
	45 ft^2	50 ft^2	50 ft^2	60 ft^2	65 ft^2
5–10	Storm	Marginal	Marginal	Marginal	Full
	45 ft^2	50 ft^2	50 ft^2	50 ft^2	60 ft^2
10–15	Mini	Mini	Storm	Marginal	Marginal
	40 ft^2	40 ft^2	45 ft^2	50 ft^2	50 ft^2
15–20	N/A	Mini	Mini	Storm	Marginal
		40 ft^2	40 ft^2	45 ft^2	50 ft^2
over 20	N/A	N/A	Mini	Mini	Storm
			40 ft^2	40 ft^2	45 ft^2

Sail Type/Area

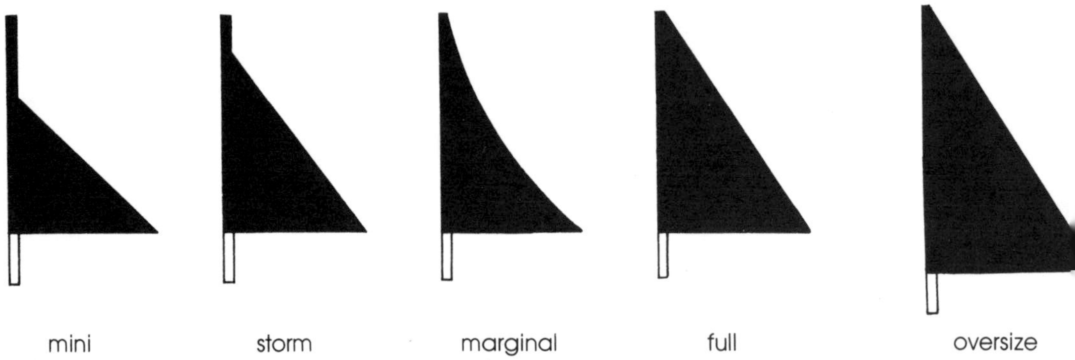

Freesailing is refreshing. It keeps you in shape and you can continue to improve every time you go out. RHONDA SMITH, TOP ALL-ROUND WOMAN FREESAILOR

CHAPTER 4
Basic Sailing

The following basic sailing manoeuvers will enable you to sail on all possible points of sail in light wind. With several hours of practice your confidence will grow and you will want to test your skills in higher winds.

Steering

The craft is steered by raking the sail either toward the bow or toward the stern. Raking the sail forward (toward the bow) heads the boat downwind (first diagram). Raking the sail aft (toward the stern) turns the boat upwind (second diagram). Raking the sail is accomplished by simple arm movements. When the rig is raked aft, the fore arm is bent and the aft arm is straight. When the rig is raked forward, the fore arm is straight and the aft arm is bent. When steering upwind, avoid pulling (sheeting) the sail in or across the wind too far as this will stall the sail.

Maintaining Course

WIND

Once the boat has been brought onto the desired course, bring the rig to a neutral or central position that holds the boat on that course. By keeping an eye on your heading, you will automatically make the adjustments of sail trim. Rake it forward slightly if the craft points above your heading, or rake it aft slightly if the craft drops below your heading.

Sailing Downwind

Sailing downwind or running with the wind is probably the trickiest point of sail. It requires a slightly different stance and an odd positioning of the rig. Sail on a beam reach.

Rake the sail forward to bear off the wind until the hull is pointing almost straight downwind.

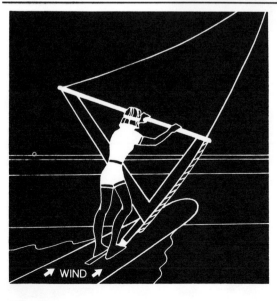

At this point the sail will become perpendicular to the hull and the wind. Your feet will be straddling the center line of the hull on either side or slightly aft of the daggerboard well and pointing toward the bow of the boat. The booms will be horizontal and in front of you.

Tacking

Being on a tack is sailing a constant course. Tacking is bringing the boat around onto a new course by turning the hull up into the wind, stepping around the front of the mast to the opposite side of the sail and bearing off onto the new course. Sail on a beam reach.

Rake the sail aft to start the hull turning up into the wind.

As the hull approaches head to wind, release your aft hand from the boom and grasp the mast.

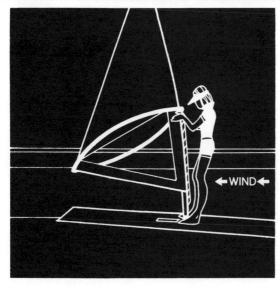

Step around to the front of the mast and square the boat up. Proceed with the five steps for getting under way.

OPPOSITE On a beam reach in
western Canada.

ABOVE Heading back to shore
before the storm breaks.

Jibing

Jibing is bringing the boat around onto a new course by turning the hull downwind and around onto the new course. Sail on a beam reach.

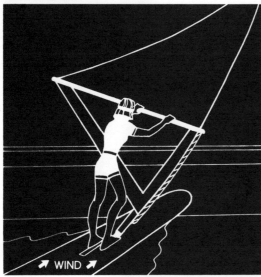

Rake the sail forward until the hull is heading straight downwind.

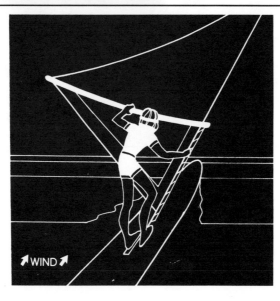

Release your fore hand from the boom and grasp the mast.

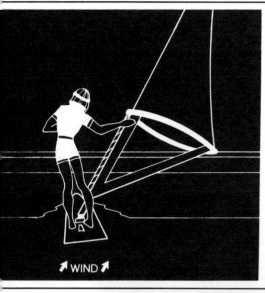

At this point, release your aft hand from the boom allowing the clew of the sail to swing around to the opposite side of the hull.

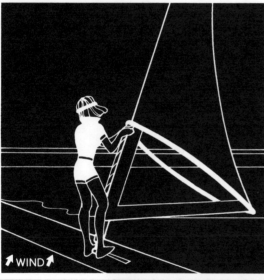

Grasp the mast with both hands and rake the sail forward and across in front of you.

Square up and proceed with the five steps for getting under way.

CHAPTER 5
High Wind Freesailing

Freesailing in high wind is the most exciting form of sailing. The sailor is as free as the wind itself, fully in control and able to fly across the waves like a slender-winged sea bird.

...ning using a high wind sail.

As the wind and boatspeed increase, there are a few small alterations that should be made to the craft. The simplest change is to flatten the sail by pulling it in tightly with the outhaul. If the wind is very strong, you will find it easier to use a smaller sail (see Diagram 2). A full-sized daggerboard will also cause a control problem; the hull will roll up onto its rails. Reducing the daggerboard area by pulling it up halfway in the daggerboard well will partially alleviate this problem. Or you can use a specially designed high wind daggerboard, which makes the craft very responsive, except when sailing upwind. (The boat cannot point as high into the wind with the smaller daggerboard. Caution must therefore be used when a powerful offshore wind is blowing.)

The manoeuvers that are used in high wind sailing are basically the same as those used in light wind sailing. The difference is that the sail develops more power from a stronger wind and you are able to execute these moves more quickly. The quicker the move is made, the sooner you will gain balance on the rig and be under way.

Getting under way in a strong wind requires good concentration, a little more muscle and faster movements. The difficulty lies in leaning back against the stronger pull of the sail and raking the rig forward far enough to bear off as you gain way. It is advisable to practise this move on land to avoid falling repeatedly when you are on the water. As you become proficient with the moves required, you will find the proper balance points and be ready to try it on the water.

You will find when you sail in high winds that the hull becomes less stable with the increased wave action and you become more dependent on the sail to keep you out of the water. The hands must move aft slightly on the booms to keep the rig balanced. If the hull tends to head upwind, rake the rig forward toward the bow as you sheet in. Think of your aft hand as an accelerator. The more you sheet in, the faster you go because of the increased power. Sheeting out spills wind from your sail and reduces the power.

...ou don't have to push a
...s pedal and you still
...t enough speed to
...tisfy a desire for going
...st. There is a great deal
... satisfaction and exhil-
...ation in matching the
...ements of wind and
...ater.

...RY TOLMAN, FREESAILING INSTRUCTOR

Getting Under Way in High Winds

Sail on a beam reach. Hold the boom with both hands and allow the sail to luff.

WIND

Rake the rig forward and across the hull.
Keep the sail luffing.

WIND

WIND

Bend both knees and sit back as you sheet in with the aft hand. Push hard on the fore foot to bear off the wind.

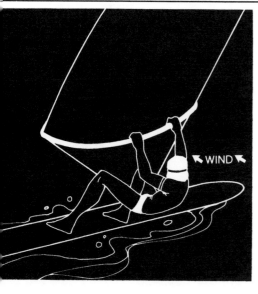

Move your hands aft on the booms and move your feet aft on the board after you are under way.

Freesailing offers me an escape that is both physically invigorating and mentally stimulating.

ROBBIE NAISH, WORLD CHAMPION

ABOVE High winds and giant waves off Hawaii.
LEFT Technique rather than strength is important in high wind freesailing.

ary Eversale, a top freestyle
ompetitor, performs a
pectacular flare.

Fast Tack

A fast tack in high wind is essentially the same as a tack done in light wind except that it is done much more quickly and the squaring up step is omitted. To counter the greater pull of the sail in stronger winds, bend your legs to lower your center of gravity. Proceed on a beam reach.

Rake the rig aft quickly, at the same time moving your aft foot further toward the stern of the hull. Under full sail power, the hull rounds up very quickly into the wind.

Move sharply around the front of the mast, releasing the aft hand.

With the new fore hand, grasp the mast and pull it immediately across in front of you without bringing the hull around to the square position.

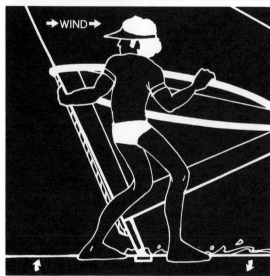

Place the aft hand three feet (one metre) back on the boom. Shift your fore hand from the mast onto the boom, one foot (30 centimetres) aft of the mast.

Fall back against the pull of the sail, pushing the bow around onto the desired heading with the fore foot. Move your feet further aft as the boat picks up speed. Moving the feet corresponds to moving the hands for balance and allows you to sail much faster.

LEFT John Boothroyd chases the camera boat.
BELOW World champion, Robbie Naish, practises in heavy wind.

downwind jibe.

Fast Jibe

Again, the fast jibe is done essentially the same way as a jibe in light wind but under full sail power is done more quickly. Proceed on a beam reach.

Rake the sail forward sharply and place your front foot forward slightly causing the boat to bear off. Be prepared to spill wind from your sail at this point by sheeting out. A sudden build-up of power on the sail will pull you forward and off-balance.

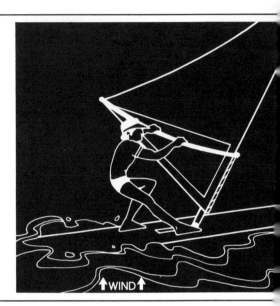

As the hull moves around downwind, pivot your aft foot and place your fore foot back toward the stern of the hull.

Pull hard on the front end of the boom and drive the ste... around.

Grasp the mast with the fore hand and release the aft hand from the boom, letting the wind flip the clew of the sail around to the opposite side of the hull.

Place your aft hand on the mast and with both hands pull the sail across in front of you.

Place the aft hand on the boom about three feet (one metre) from the mast.

Shift your fore hand from the mast to the boom and sheet in, continuing to rake the rig aft until the hull comes around onto the desired heading. Move your feet ahead slightly as you get under way.

Water Start

When sailing in strong winds, you will sometimes find yourself in the water on the windward side with your feet still on the hull and the sail a few inches above the water's surface. Recovery from this position is possible without having to climb back onto the hull and without having to hoist the sail.

Push up with the fore hand to raise the mast and sail higher into the wind, sheet in a bit to build power in the sail and rake the rig forward to keep the hull square. Spread your feet wide over the daggerboard area to keep the hull drifting sideways. When a strong gust hits the sail, sheet in to develop enough power to lift you from the water. Rake the rig forward and set your new course.

→ WIND →

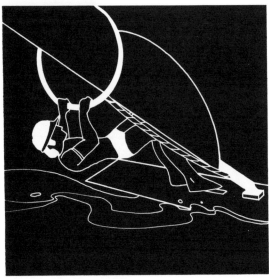

Diagram 2. Sail Choice for Advanced Sailing

Sailor's Weight in Pounds	50–100	100–125	125–150	150–175	175+
2–10	Marginal 50 ft²	Full 60 ft²	Oversize 65 ft²	Oversize 65 ft²	Oversize 65 ft²
10–20	Storm 45 ft²	Marginal 50 ft²	Full 60 ft²	Full 60 ft²	Oversize 65 ft²
20–25	Mini 40 ft²	Storm 45 ft²	Marginal 50 ft²	Full 60 ft²	Full 60 ft²
25–30	N/A	Mini 40 ft²	Mini 45 ft²	Storm 50 ft²	Marginal 60 ft²
over 30	N/A	N/A	Mini 45 ft²	Mini 45 ft²	Storm 50 ft²

Sail Type/Area

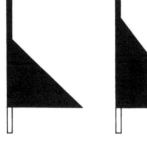

mini   storm   marginal   full   oversize

Flare

Also known as a "wheelie," the flare is a good way to slow the hull quickly and initiate a fast jibe. This manoeuver is spectacular when done in a strong wind.

From a beam reach, rake the sail forward, bear off and strive for top speed. As the hull comes into line with the wind, kick the hull forward by stepping quickly toward the stern.

Pull the boom down hard toward you as the bow rises. Then ease your pull on the boom and step forward. The hull will flatten out and continue downwind. Hold the rig in toward you until the hull stops. Leaning the rig laterally at this point initiates a fast tack or jibe. Step forward quickly on the hull once it has stopped.

After you have experienced the sensation of high wind sailing, light winds will no longer present a challenge. High wind sailing is, of course, more physically taxing than light wind sailing. To reduce sailor fatigue Hawaiian freesailors invented the harness.

CHAPTER 6
Harness Sailing

Once you have mastered the basics and find yourself limited by burning hands and forearms you are ready for harness sailing. The harness is a jacket-like device worn by the freesailor, which attaches him to the rig. The sailor's body weight, used to counter the pull of the sail, is 75 per cent supported by the harness, leaving the hands and arms free to make the continuous adjustments in sail trim. Instead of 110 yard (100 metre) rides, freesailors in Hawaii are now making 90 mile (150 kilometre) trips, thanks to the energy-conserving harness.

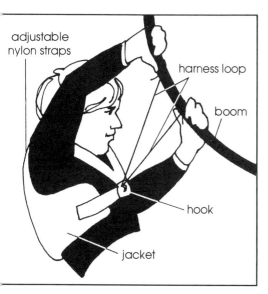

adjustable nylon straps

harness loop

boom

hook

jacket

Figure 6. Harness

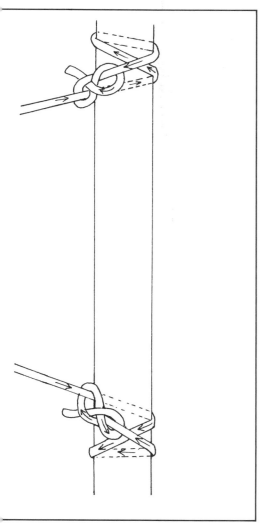

Figure 7. Half-hitch figure-eight knots

Parts of a Harness

The harness consists of the jacket that you wear and two ropes, one attached to each boom.

The harness jacket is a foam padded, nylon or dacron jacket designed to support the upper body comfortably. Nylon webbing straps over the shoulders adjust the height of the harness hook, which hooks onto a rope loop. Another strap across the chest closes the jacket through the hook with a quick release clip. The hook can be positioned pointing up or down.

The harness loops are attached to the booms using simple half-hitch figure-eight knots or more sophisticated straps. The straps offer less interference to hand movement along the booms.

Setting Up the Harness

After you have rigged your sail, pick it up on land and trim it to the wind. This works well in a location with good exposure to steady wind.

When your hands have balanced the pull of the sail on the boom, you will have a good indication of where the loops should be tied. The ends of the lines should be attached just inside the hand positions. This will create a loop roughly 20 inches (50 centimetres) long. The maximum amount of play in the loop will depend on your arm length and personal preference. Experimentation will determine the best loop placement for a given wind condition. The basic rule to follow is: the higher the wind, the farther back the loops are placed from the mast. In an extremely high wind, the front end of a loop will be up to 30 inches (75 centimetres) from the mast.

When tying the loops on the booms, make sure that the knots or straps are tight and will maintain their positions. The half-hitch figure-eight knot when tied correctly allows easy adjustment while sailing. Simply push up on the knots with the thumbs to loosen the hitches and slide the loops along to the desired position. Hook in, and your body weight clinches the knots. Straps tend to hold their positions very well once they are tightened.

Adjusting the Jacket

Most harness jackets allow hook height adjustments to be made by varying the length of the shoulder straps. The hook should sit between or slightly below the pectoral muscles.

The quick release closure makes it possible to adjust the jacket to accommodate the added bulk of a wetsuit. A snug fit, which restricts breathing and movement is not desirable, nor should the hook hang loosely. A loosely hanging hook makes hooking in difficult.

When tying the booms to the mast, ensure that shoulder height is maintained. This position allows for the easiest hooking in and out.

Use of the Harness

Being hooked to your rig takes some getting used to, and initial attempts at sailing with a harness can be unnerving. As in learning anything new on your freesail craft, first tries should be made in light onshore winds with your rig on dry ground.

Once your booms are rigged with the harness loops, pick up your rig and trim it to the wind to simulate a sailing situation.

With the Hook Down.   Pull the boom toward you and down while raising your upper body as high as possible. This positions the hook above the loop ready to hook in. You hook onto the loop by lifting up on the boom and lowering your body. Extend your arms slowly until your body weight is countering the pull of the sail. Slide the boom either forward or backward until an evenly balanced pull is felt on the harness.

To unhook, pull the boom toward you and down. The loop will drop from the hook. Extend your arms again and you will be sailing under manual power. Repeat this procedure until you can do it without having to look down at the hook and loop.

With the Hook Up.   Pull the boom toward you and up, while bending your legs slightly. This will position the loop above the upturned hook. Stand erect and lower the boom. The loop will fall into the hook. Extend your arms slowly until your body weight counters the pull of the sail and slide the boom forward or backward until the rig is balanced.

To unhook, pull the boom toward you and up as you bend slightly at the knee. A more conscious effort is required to unhook with the hook up and the sailor should be well acquainted with the procedure before trying it on the water.

Top freesailors prefer to have the hook pointing up. The advantages of the hook up position are twofold: accidental hooking in is less likely and the loop stays in the hook while sail trim adjustments are being made.

Once you have familiarized yourself with hooking in and out on land, you are ready to try harness sailing on the water. Best results will be achieved in a light wind on nearly flat water. First attempts on the water should be made while sailing upwind.

Sailing downwind with the harness unhooked.

Tips

If the pull on the arms is decidedly one-sided, move the loop in that direction. That is, if you have to pull hard on the fore hand to keep yourself balanced, the loop is probably too far back on the boom. Moving the loop forward a few inches by readjusting the position of the knot will bring you into balance.

Learning to use a harness is easier if the loop is positioned slightly forward of the central position on the boom. A loop placed this way will make it easier to sheet out by spilling wind from the sail.

Points of Sail While Using the Harness

The harness is used to best advantage while sailing upwind. The strain on the arms is lessened dramatically. Race your friends to a far shore and back or take a lunch in a pack attached to your harness and go even farther afield.

The sailor does not need to be hooked in while running downwind because strain is minimal on this heading. However, sometimes the hook will snag on the loop and throw the sailor off-balance. To avoid hooking in while running downwind, slide the front knot forward toward the mast, pulling the loop tightly against the boom.

Using the Harness in Strong Winds

As your skill improves, you will be ready to try sailing with your harness in stronger winds. Bearing off onto a reach in high winds gives you the feeling of being instantly accelerated to near wind speed—very exciting in 25 knots, but be careful of the "launch."

Getting launched from the freesail craft in strong, gusty winds is a somewhat unsettling experience, to say the least! If the rig is raked too far forward while you are hooked in, it becomes very difficult to counter the pull of the sail against the drag of the hull. The sailor is pulled off-balance, launching him over the bow of the craft. Care must be taken to land as gently as possible to prevent damage to the mast, booms or your body. The launch closely resembles pitch-poling in a catamaran sailboat or a good tumble on skis.

Continual use of the harness loops in strong winds will quickly wear out the loop line. Always inspect the line before going out on the water. Badly frayed lines should be replaced. By using an overlength line and varying the tail at either end, loop life can be substantially prolonged.

CHAPTER 7

Competitive Freesailing

The excitement of competitive freesailing is attracting sailors to local, national and international regattas in ever increasing numbers.

"The great challenge of racing is head to head combat and racing people in your own weight class. You have to decide where to tack, which side to sail on and whether to go with a windshift or not."

ALEX AGUERA, NORTH AMERICAN MEDIUMWEIGHT CHAMPION

In Canada, small communities of freesailors have sprung up within the past few years. Regattas take place in Eastern Canada nearly every weekend during the summer months. (In 1977, Collingwood, Ontario, hosted the North American Championships.) In Western Canada, Whistler, British Columbia, is one of the most popular areas for racing. Local regattas provide novices with a chance to learn competitive freesailing and experienced sailors with a chance to practise for the final event of the season, the Canadian Windsurfing Championships. This regatta is held yearly and attracts competitors from across the country.

In the United States, each freesailing community holds regattas for local fleet members. In addition, each section of the United States is divided into districts which hold district regattas. These events culminate in the North American Championships. Freesailors from all districts are invited to attend, including Canadian sailors. Hawaiian freesailors hold an open class regatta each year in which boards of any design can be used. Recently a professional long-distance race was introduced with cash prizes for the winners.

Freesailing competitions are also popular in Europe, where there are over one hundred races every weekend. Europeans must place in the top three in their local regattas to participate in the European Championships. The winners of this regatta go on to the World Championships.

Since 1973 freesailors from all over the world have gathered in a tropical country during October or November to participate in the Worlds. This championship has been dominated by Robbie Naish whom most freesailors would call the best Olympic triangle racer in the world. He won his first world championship at the age of thirteen in 1976 at Emerald Beach, Nassau, and is a three time world champion. The following pages will show you how to become a good competitor, if not a Robbie Naish.

A Race with Your Friends

Before you and your friends head for the local regatta, you may want to practise first in your own race. The standard course, which has been adopted from sailboat racing, is the Olympic triangle course.

Olympic Triangle Course   On an Olympic triangle course, the sailor sails the three main points of sail: a beat, a reach and a run. The first leg of the course, called the weather leg, begins below the triangle course on a starting line situated between two marks placed square to the wind. (These marks can be old, spray-painted Javex bottles, painted inner tubes or buoy balls.) After the ten minute starting sequence has been completed, the boats tack upwind to the windward or weather mark. The usual practice is to round the marks without touching them to port, that is leaving them on the port side of the craft.

The second leg of the course is called the starboard broad reach. The boats sail downwind on a broad reach to the reaching or jibing mark. Here the boats jibe around the mark leaving it to port and proceed on the third leg. The third leg is a port broad reach on the opposite tack toward the leeward mark, which is situated just above the start line.

Rounding the leeward mark, the boats head back upwind on the second beat and the fourth leg of the course. After rounding the windward mark for the second time, the fifth leg of the course is a run straight downwind to the leeward mark, which again is rounded to port. The sixth leg is the final beat to the finish line, located upwind of the windward mark.

A boat has finished the course as soon as the bow touches the line. It must cross the line and clear the finish area immediately to make way for following boats.

To simplify this course, the start/finish line can be one and the same, placed halfway between the windward and leeward marks. This also shortens the course by half of the first and last beats.

In most regattas a committee boat is used by the judges, who give the starting sequence, watch for fouls, etc. However, a small group of freesailors can avoid the need for a committee boat by using a rabbit start. In a rabbit start one boat crosses in front of the other boats or fleet on a starboard tack. The individual boats in the fleet start when the starter (rabbit) boat passes them. The sailor in the starter boat must jibe before sailing a course to the windward mark so that he doesn't have an advantage over the other boats.

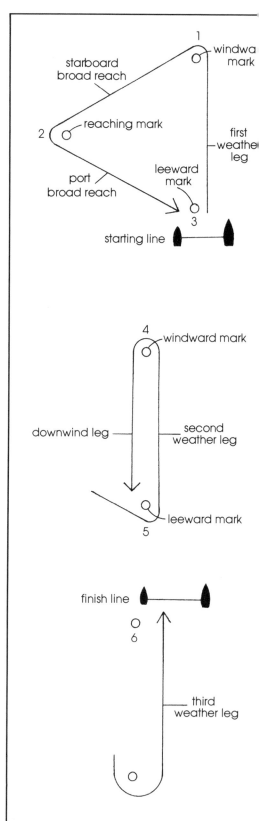

Figure 8. Olympic triangle course

Starting a Race   There are a number of variations to the starting procedure. We will discuss a format that is useful for small regattas.

A line consisting of two marks set square to the wind comprises the start line of a sailing race. Enough room must be allowed between these marks to accommodate all the boats in the fleet. The race committee should be in a boat at the starboard end of the line, unless a rabbit start is being used.

In most sailing races, a ten minute start sequence is used. For your race, however, a five minute sequence will probably be sufficient to prepare the fleet for the start.

A watch is very helpful to guarantee a good start. At the precise moment when the start sequence begins, you should note the time. This ensures that you are physically in the right place and mentally prepared for the final signal. You can also time the committee and make sure that the starting sequence is being handled correctly. In large regattas, if a sailor finds that the starting sequence is incorrect, he has the right to protest to the race committee.

There are a number of sailing watches on the market. The most practical and economical are the lightweight, plastic encased digital watches with a stop watch feature. These are available at approximately one-fifth the price of specialized sailing watches.

After all the boats have lined up along the start line, the race committee should simultaneously hoist a red flag and sound an audible signal (either a gunshot or a horn blast) to begin the five minute countdown to the start. Sailors should set their watches at this signal. Three and one-half minutes into the sequence the red flag is dropped. At four minutes (one minute to go) a blue flag is raised. Sailors should again check their watches. With thirty seconds to go the blue flag is dropped. On Go, the red flag is raised and the audible signal is given to start the race.

Any boats over the line early have their numbers called on a loudhailer and must round either end of the start line and start again or be disqualified. If too many boats are over early to call individual numbers, a general recall signal is sounded (three blasts) and the full five minute sequence begins again.

Downwind leg of a one design class race.

Preparing for a Local Competition

When you feel you are ready to race in a local regatta, ask your dealer for details of regatta schedules and association membership forms. He can be most helpful in getting you started.

Don't be worried about your level of expertise. Most regattas hold races for more advanced racers (the A fleet) and for beginning racers (the B fleet). Nor do you have to worry about your size or strength. Each competitor is usually placed in a weight class. Weight classes consist of lightweights, mediumweights, medium heavyweights and heavyweights. The cut-off points depend on the number of people in the regatta and the distribution of weight. There is sometimes a special class for women; however, if there aren't enough women competitors to form a fleet, they race with the men.

Where once athletic, long-time freesailors dominated most events, conventional small boat sailors are now turning their talents to freesail competitions and are proving that brawn is not necessarily required to win a race. A knowledge of racing tactics and skillful boat handling usually add up to victory.

Rules   To compete successfully, the freesailor should have a good understanding of the rules regulating sailboat racing. These regulations are designed to establish right of way of one boat over another and to prevent collisions. Tactics, which are based on the rules, are obviously very important in racing. The better your knowledge of the regulations, the better your chances of winning a race.

The rules can be studied in the International Yacht Racing Union book or in a book on sailing tactics such as Eric Twiname's **The Rules Book.** As your racing experience grows, you will begin to understand the rules more fully and to be able to recognize instances where they can be used to your advantage over other boats. Here are a few basic rules to help keep you out of trouble on your first race.

Fighting for clean air while sailing to the reaching mark.

1. Port/Starboard Boats.   When two boats on opposite tacks are approaching a common point, the starboard tack boat has right of way. The port boat must either give way and go behind, or tack onto starboard and keep clear.

2. Windward/Leeward.   When two boats on the same tack are overlapped, the leeward boat has "luffing rights" over the windward boat. The leeward boat can head up, and the windward boat must keep clear. When an overlapped windward boat reaches a position where its daggerboard is even with the leeward boat's mast, the sailor calls "mast abeam" and the leeward boat loses its luffing rights. The overtaking boat (windward here) must keep clear however.

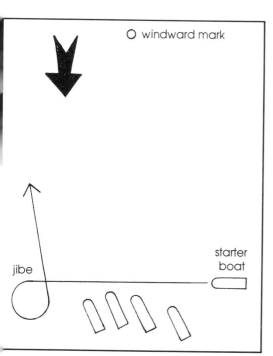

O windward mark

jibe

starter boat

Figure 9. Rabbit start

3. Room at Marks. When two boats approach a mark, and the inside boat has an overlap on the leading boat at the moment that boat's bow enters the two boat length circle around the mark, the following boat calls for "buoy room" and must be given ample room to round the mark.

4. Room to Pass Obstructions. When two boats on the same tack approach an obstruction, the right of way boat cannot force the other boat into that obstruction. The right of way boat must waive those rights and allow the other to clear the obstruction.

5. Tacking and Jibing. A boat must keep clear of others while tacking or jibing. While the sail luffs during tacking or jibing a boat has no rights over others.

6. Ample Room and Opportunity. If a boat suddenly achieves right of way over another by tacking onto starboard or becoming leeward boat, the other boat must be given ample room and opportunity to keep clear.

7. Touching a Mark is a Foul. The mark must be re-rounded.

8. Penalties. A boat that fouls another can exonerate itself from that foul by doing a 720° turn as soon as possible after the infringement. The fouled boat should notify the culprit of his intention to protest. A boat has no rights while doing a 720°, or while re-rounding marks, including start line marks.

Boat Handling Boat handling skills are very important in competition. You must be able to remain in control of your craft in all situations and derive maximum power from the wind and water conditions. With the confidence gained through experience and practice, you will soon find yourself first at the windward mark.

To brush up your skills prior to a race, practise the basic manoeuvers of tacking, jibing, sailing close hauled, and running downwind.

Sailing to Weather Successful sailing close to the wind should also be practised before a race. A skillful sailor will be able to show you just how high you can point.

Three things to keep in mind when racing upwind are:
1. Keep maximum power on the sail. This you sense through your hands. You will feel if the sail is pulling hard or not.
2. Point as high as possible into the wind. Keep your eye on the windward mark and tack on all wind shifts that are advantageous.
3. Maintain good boat speed. Don't pinch or head too high up into the wind, to the point where you lose boat speed.

Racing Techniques   Proper technique is crucial to windward performance. Concentration is required to hold the craft on the best angle of attack when approaching the windward mark.

In light air, the rig should be held as upright as possible and trimmed closely to or over the hull's center line. By keeping the arms and legs locked, a tight link between sailor and craft is established and slight wind increases will be transferred directly to boat speed. Placing the feet as closely as comfort allows to the daggerboard area minimizes unwanted changes in direction.

As the windspeed increases a number of changes in technique must be made. Hands and harness loops improve balance when moved aft slightly in an average wind or radically in a heavy wind. With the center of effort moving aft, the feet must also shift to a position just behind the daggerboard well. By placing the feet closer to the edge of the hull, it becomes easier to hold the craft level. There is a tendency for the hull to rail up when driven hard, and it is advisable when this happens to reduce the daggerboard area by pulling the daggerboard halfway up in the well.

Locking in or keeping your body rigid can also turn gusts in high winds to your advantage. You must, however, be prepared to move quickly in response to shifts or lulls.

When tacking, try to maintain speed onto the new heading. Trim the sail as quickly as possible and avoid excessive bearing off while getting under way. Long tacks are advisable in light wind as tacking takes too much time, unless a shift in the wind makes a new tack advantageous. You have only so much wind to work with so make the most of it.

The Competition

The Start   A good start is always essential but not necessarily easy to achieve. With fifty to one hundred boats on the start line, it takes no imagination to envision the chaos that often develops. To avoid being late at the start, familiarize yourself before the race with the starting procedures chosen by the race committee. Check in early at the committee boat and sail along the line to establish your preferred starting position. Before the ten minute signal, sail a couple of tacks toward the windward mark. If time permits, sail a leg of the course and with another boat try opposite tacks to determine which side of the course is favored. All this information will be highly valuable in determining your tactics for the race.

Be near the committee boat when the start sequence is being counted down to allow for an accurate watch setting.

Once the start sequence has begun, check the line a second time to see if the initial start plan is still valid. Observing experienced sailors will definitely help. (Try following one in the race, being careful of course to keep out of his or her way. Start just behind where he starts, tack when he tacks and watch his reactions at each mark.)

Two sailors tack to the windward mark. One competitor has chosen a starboard tack and the other a port tack.

Check the daggerboard for weeds and take a quick last minute look at all fittings on the craft. They should be okay if you checked them on the beach.

On most starts the starboard end will be favored because the boat closest to this mark has starboard tack right of way over all other boats. However, if the port end of the line is set more upwind than the starboard end, the port end becomes more advantageous. These areas are prone to chaos, though, and unless you have excellent boat handling abilities should be avoided. An unnecessary fall with ten seconds to go loses friends and the race. In your first races try to start from a less crowded position where you will have clean air (wind that is not affected by the movement of other boats) and fewer boats to contend with.

It is desirable to have some speed when crossing the line but this is not always possible as most of the boats will be to the right on the starting line, leaving no gaps to power through when the gun goes off. Always try to be in the front row of boats because the dirty air from the sails upwind makes it difficult to gain way.

Rounding Marks The variations of boat positions and the rules that apply to each situation at a mark are seemingly endless. Knowing the rules inside and out and being able to see their application instantly obviously helps in a race, however, all that

I will never become a great racer but the sport is so exhilarating that I try. Even when you are standing in light winds you have to use all your muscles.

GRETA SCHEFFTER, NEW ENGLAND
FREESAILOR

ABOVE Rounding the
windward mark.
LEFT Ontario racer, Quentin
Pollock, on the windward leg
of a course.

cers in Collingwood,
ntario, head for the
aching mark.

takes time and experience. In the meantime, a few simple points should be kept in mind.

Always come to the windward mark in a position that gives you the right of way. On courses where marks are rounded to port, get on a final starboard approach a good distance from the mark, aiming high of the mark to allow for wind shifts and any boats that acquire inside rights. By coming in a little above the mark, you can always bear off and gain extra speed while rounding. If the wind is strong enough to permit planing conditions on the reach, reduce your daggerboard area once you have rounded to allow better hull control. If balance is a problem on the reach or run, try kneeling down on one knee or both if the water is rough. This will prevent an unwanted fall.

Try to come around the reaching and leeward marks without slipping too far downwind. Come onto the mark wide, initiate the jibe early and pass as closely below the mark as possible. With a lot of boats following upwind, the air is not very clean and can cause a sloppy jibe. Be prepared to leave sufficient room for boats with overlap rights.

Finishing   Try to finish on the favored end of the line on a starboard tack. Once across the line, sail clear of the area before celebrating or bemoaning your result. This is a simple act of courtesy that will be appreciated by competitors and race committee alike.

Long-distance and Slalom Racing

In addition to Olympic triangle racing, you may want to try long-distance or slalom racing.

A long-distance course is six miles (ten kilometres) or over in length. A variation of the Olympic triangle course, it often consists of an upwind leg, a downwind leg and two reaching legs.

The race is started from a Le Mans start. All the competitors line up on the beach with their boards placed in the water. At the sound of the gun, they run to their boards, hoist their sails and get under way. Just as in Olympic triangle racing, there are favored ends of the start line. When picking a starting position or area to place your board, take the same things into consideration that you would at the start of an Olympic triangle race—the direction of the wind, location of the first mark, etc.

There are a few points to keep in mind if you plan to long-distance race. A harness is indispensable and you should learn how to use one. Endurance and the ability to maintain concentration over a long period of time are essential. To build up your strength for long-distance racing go for long sails with your friends.

Slalom racing is similar to the dual slalom in snow skiing. The course consists of two lines of three buoys lined up opposite each

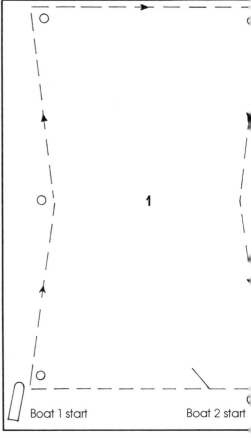

Boat 1 start   Boat 2 start

Figure 10. Slalom course.

other. Two competitors sail through the markers in a prescribed fashion (see Figure 10) at the same time. Touching the marks is legal in slalom racing, but sailing right of way rules apply. This type of race requires excellent jibing and tacking skills and tactical abilities.

If there is a violation of the method prescribed for going through the marks, a competitor is disqualified. Freesailors who plan to slalom race should carefully study the proper way to go through the marks. People fail in slalom simply because they don't take the time to learn where they are supposed to go.

The starting sequence for a slalom race consists of five or ten minute warnings. A minute gun or horn blast is sounded and the sequence is audibly counted down from the thirty second point. One freesailor starts at the port end of the line and the other at the starboard end. The ends they start at are decided by the race committee. The person who finishes the slalom course first without any mistakes is the winner.

Both long-distance and slalom racing are included in most regattas along with Olympic triangle racing and freestyle competitions. The scores of a competitor who competes in all four events are combined to make up a cumulative score. The competitor with the highest score is declared the best all-round sailor at a regatta.

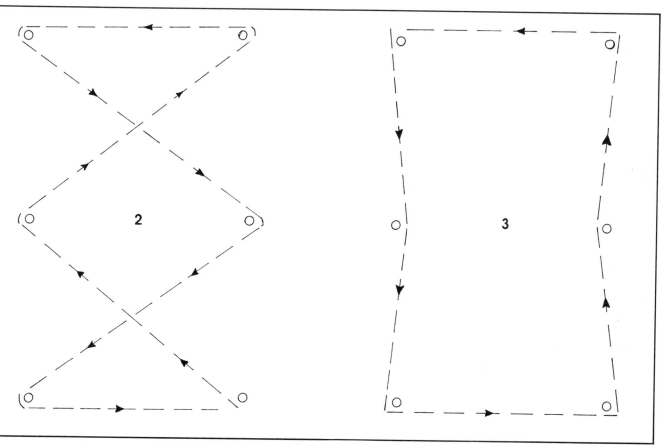

(The course is followed by boat one in the diagram. Boat two sails a path that is the mirror image of boat one's.)

CHAPTER 8

Wave Surfing

After you have acquired the ability to tack and jibe quickly in rough water and high wind, you will be ready to experience the ultimate thrill in small craft sailing—wave surfing.

ABOVE Hugh England uses smaller sail while wave surf in high wind.

OPPOSITE Riding ahead of t white water.

A combination of sailing and surfing was what the originators of the freesail craft had in mind when they conceived the sport. Sail power has obvious advantages over paddling between the waves with the hands. Instead of waiting as a surfer does for the perfect wave, the freesailor is continually moving through the surf, putting himself in the ideal place to catch the best ride. Every freesailor has felt the acceleration caused by even the smallest waves on lakes. As the waves become larger, acceleration increases and an exhilarating ride is prolonged.

Before you attempt wave surfing a few tips and notes of caution. Wave surfing is not recommended for the newcomer to the sport. A spill in breaking surf on a freesail craft can be hazardous to both body and equipment.

When you are proficient at freesailing, the best way to introduce yourself to wave surfing is to find a location where the swells have no white water breaking on their crests and are about three feet (one metre) in height. Such conditions can be found on large lakes or some distance offshore in coastal locations. Once you have familiarized yourself with the higher speed of wave surfing and the apparent wind factor (see below), you will be ready to try larger waves and to experience the thrill of white water.

Never attempt to surf in shorebreak, the waves breaking on the beach. This is extremely dangerous water. A hard fall can result in broken booms and mast, a torn sail and injuries to you.

Apparent Wind

An interesting phenomenon takes place as a boat's speed increases and approaches the speed of the wind. A new wind direction and velocity is created called apparent wind. One of the best explanations of apparent wind that we have found is in Stephen Colgate's book, **Colgate's Basic Sailing Theory**. He defines apparent wind as "the resultant wind derived from the wind produced by the boat moving through the air and the wind produced by nature—the 'true wind.'" He gives as an example a car heading north with a ten mile per hour easterly wind blowing. The wind will hit the right side of a passenger's face. As the car's speed increases, the passenger doesn't feel two different winds, one on the side of his face and one on the front, but a resultant wind coming from an angle forward of the true wind.

There are four basic thoughts to keep in mind when encountering apparent wind for the first time. The apparent wind always comes from a point forward of the true wind unless the true wind is astern or ahead. The second point is that the apparent wind lessens in velocity as the true wind comes aft. Third, a small change in true wind direction when it is well aft makes for a large change in apparent wind direction. Finally, when sailing on a beam reach or close hauled, the apparent wind has a higher speed than the true wind.

When bearing off in high wind, acceleration continues until the craft is running almost dead downwind. Beyond this point, apparent wind decreases as acceleration is slowed by hull drag, until the sail is affected only by the real wind, which at this point comes from directly astern and is diminished by the speed that the craft moves with the wind.

Apparent wind becomes a major factor in wave surfing. With the added acceleration of the wave, the apparent wind increases very quickly. It takes some time to get used to keeping the sail trimmed correctly to maintain balance.

How to Wave Surf

On a beam reach, the sailor sights a wave, ahead and slightly upwind, and bears off down its face as it rises up under the hull. A freesailor must be careful not to outrun the wind. Bearing off too quickly too far will move the hull ahead of the wind causing the sail to become backwinded. This creates a balance problem. The sailor is usually knocked backward into the water by the sail. In higher wind, balance is more easily maintained.

The best conditions for wave surfing are found, of course, in coastal ocean locations. Not only are large waves a regular occurrence, but often the wind direction will vary from that of the wave travel. It is in such conditions that apparent wind can be used to the best advantage. The faster the craft accelerates down the wave, the stronger the apparent wind becomes. The result is a very fast ride.

Beginners should learn to wave surf in light winds and on small waves.

CHAPTER 9

Wave Jumping

"Air time" is a popular cry of freestyle skiers and is now being introduced to the sailing world. Pictures of freesail crafts suspended mysteriously above the water are appearing everywhere and explanations are in demand. How did they get up there? Like the skier who approaches a mogul on a ski slope, skis up it and shoots out into the air, the freesailor approaches an oncoming wave, sails up its face and becomes airborne as the wave passes underneath.

OPPOSITE Cort Larned, a top
American freesailor,
suspended above the water
in a breathtaking jump.

BELOW Expert wave jumpers,
Colin Perry and Mike Horgan,
are able to leap 16 feet (5
metres) under ideal
conditions.

The main requirements for wave jumping are lots of wind (at least 20 knots), footstraps on the hull and a good breaking offshore surf. In some locations, wind and wave directions are often not parallel. These areas offer the best jumping conditions because the angle formed between the wind and wave directions sometimes approaches 90° — ideal for the beam or broad reach needed to ascend a wave.

Wakes from large motorboats are also fun to jump and a co-operative driver can provide hours of enjoyment for the skilled and adventurous freesailor. Unwary boat drivers are astounded when freesailors approach their stern wakes and fly seven feet (two metres) into the air. They are even more surprised at successful landings!

The best waves for jumping can be found on the Hawaiian Islands of Oahu and Maui. Local conditions at Kailua, Haleiwa, Kuilima and Diamond Head make it difficult to stay on the water. At Hukipa on Maui there are perfect conditions for jumps on seven to nine foot (two to three metre) waves.

Footstraps

Sailors in Kailua, Hawaii, decided after many aborted leaps that a way was needed to keep themselves attached to their boats. The solution came in the form of neoprene wrapped, nylon webbing straps. The straps resemble the fittings on the back of a slalom waterski. Two pairs are attached on either side of the daggerboard area to take the fore feet and three more pairs are added toward the stern. This arrangement allows the sailor to maintain contact with the hull in a variety of sailing situations. First-time jumpers should place their feet loosely in the footstraps so that they can be released quickly and safely in the event of a fall.

A word of caution is needed here. Remember that wave jumping is for the competent freesailor. Once you have gone through all the steps in this book and feel that you are highly proficient at them, then you might be ready for wave jumping. However, don't attempt it without instruction from experienced freesailors. Ask them if you are ready for wave jumping and, most important of all, listen to their advice.

Making a Jump

The sailor must be very aware and confident when wave jumping. Dropping the rig in front of a breaking wave can result in damaged equipment. Jumping should be done only with strong, small high wind daggerboards that permit fast sailing and that withstand the impact of landing.

A breaking wave or swell diminishes in size from the curl, where the wave is cresting and the wave face is vertical, to a shallow slope of smooth water. Initial jumps should be attempted at this smaller end of the wave. Jumps will be low but chances of

Getting airborne is a great feeling. You go along in 20 knots of wind, hit a wave, which is just like a ramp, and wait in anticipation to leave the water. When you are airborne there is a quiet feeling.

MIKE WALTZ, TWO-TIME NORTH AMERICAN LIGHT CLASS CHAMPION

This jumper is in good form as he prepares to land.

successful landings will be better. Once skill and confidence have been built, you can move along the wave to a position where you gain the greatest height from a vertical take-off. Shallower slopes will give longer jumps with less altitude.

Pick your spot and sail with maximum speed on a beam or broad reach up the face of the wave. To set the sail horizontal for the best "flight" control, lean back as the craft ascends the wave and prepare to rake the sail forward as much as you can. (In other words, try to bear off as far as possible at take-off. This maintains forward motion and sets you up for a good landing.) As the crest is reached and the bow of your board comes up into the wind, pull up on the forward footstrap, lifting the windward rail up to present the hull flat onto the wind as it becomes airborne. This guarantees your take-off. Allow full body extension for better balance in the air. Control is maintained by using the sail as a wing.

When the stern of the craft begins to descend, feel for good balance on the sail. Keeping the sail full of air provides stability and softens your landing. Absorb the impact of landing with a slight flexing of the knees and lean back to pull the sail fully onto the wind. Sail to the next wave, tack quickly and surf it in.

Wave jumping is a natural high. It's like harnessing two mother natures—the wind and the surf. Riding the wave in and jumping it on the way out is fantastic.

DOUG HUNT, FLORIDA FREESAILOR

ABOVE Doug Hunt, a Florida freesailor, leans back as his craft ascends the wave.

OPPOSITE An Australian wave jumper with a custom-made high performance board.

Freestyle Sailing

Light wind freestyle or trick sailing involves sail position variations and acrobatic body movements. With stronger wind and more power on the sail, the hull can be put through a number of exciting figures.

LEFT Cort Larned sailing on leeward side of the sail.

OPPOSITE Top European freesailor, Sigi Hoffman, demonstrates the creativit freestyle.

Most freestyle freesailing has evolved through experimentation or accident, with no rules governing creativity. Many freesailors try tricks to amuse themselves or an audience on the shore. The ten standard tricks on the following pages will help you start your own routine. In the process of learning them, you may even invent a few tricks of your own!

Here are several points to keep in mind when trick sailing. Tricks are easiest to learn in light wind but can with practice be done in strong wind. Rail rides and the body dip require more wind to be executed correctly. Lightweight booms and a tight rig are essential, and remember, always practise on dry land first.

1. Sailing on the Leeward Side of the Sail   On a beam reach, move around the mast and stand on the leeward side, facing the sail and holding the boom. Turn your body 180°. You will be sailing in the same direction, but your back will be to the sail.

2. Sailing Clew First   Jibe the boat but don't flip the sail over onto the other tack. You will be sailing along with the hull pointing forward and the sail backward.

3. Sail 360   Sail on a beam reach. Push the clew of the sail to windward or leeward, then holding the same boom, walk around the mast base, rotating the sail a full 360°. This trick can also be done on the leeward side of the sail.

4. Hull 360   Sail on a beam reach. Turn the hull up into the wind and around a full 360° by holding the sail raked aft. This turns the hull around rather than the sail. The sailor stays in a stationary position.

ABOVE Canadian freesailor Fraser Black sailing inside the booms.

BELOW LEFT Hull 360.

BELOW RIGHT Rail ride.

ᴏᴠᴇ Duck tack.

ɢʜᴛ A couple practise their
ᴇstyle routine.

A variation of sailing inside the booms.

5. Sailing Inside the Booms   Slide up inside the booms and rest your arms on top of them. Steer the hull in the same way as you would when sailing outside the booms.

6. Pirouette   Tip the sail to windward and luff it in a balanced position. Release the boom, pirouette by turning your body a full 360° and grab the same boom again when you have completed the pirouette.

7. Pirouette Tack   Pirouette once or twice around the front of the mast as you tack.

8. Rail Ride   Sail on a beam reach, flip the hull up on its edge and stand on it. Hook your fore foot under the windward rail and rest your shin on it. Then place your other foot on the top side of the rail. Sail frontward, backward and inside the booms.

9. Duck Tack   Hold the hull up into the wind. Instead of walking around the front of the mast to tack, duck under the sail and grab the opposite boom. Try a pirouette while ducking under the sail.

10. Body Dip   Sailing fast on a broad reach, drag your legs in the water while maintaining balance on the sail. Sheet out and drag your body under the water with your head above the surface. To regain your original position, sheet in and pull yourself up.

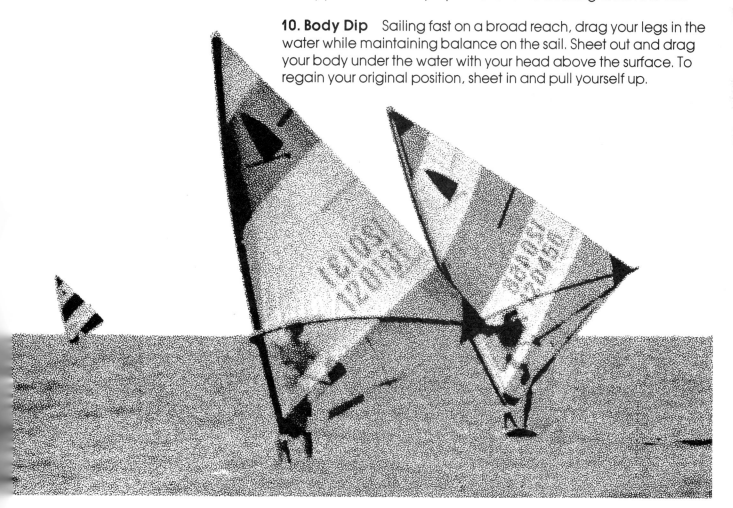

CHAPTER 11

Selecting Equipment

With a number of different freesail crafts on the market to choose from, you must decide what you want in terms of product quality. We recommend the purchase of a high-quality brand name board. Some manufacturerers have hastily assembled crafts to capitalize on the recent popularity of the sport. These boards may be cheaper but when it comes to quality they suffer. Reputable brand name boards have withstood the test of time and are much more durable than the quickly produced crafts. They can be serviced readily by dealers and stock parts such as universal joints, masts, skegs and daggerboards are easily obtainable.

Whether you want to buy a new or used board depends upon the amount of money you want to spend and your freesailing needs. A freesailor who wants to become a competitive racer will have different requirements than a person who wants to sail strictly for fun. A beginning sailor's needs will differ from the needs of an experienced sailor who wants to take up wave jumping, and an ocean sailor will require a different board than a lake sailor.

Competitive Freesail Boards

The future racer should first decide if he wants to race one design brand name boards or wants to race open class boats. In one design racing, racers compete on identical equipment and all the boards carry the same brand name. No modifications to the board or existing rig are allowed. Windsurfer® and Windglider® boards are the number one and number two boards for one design racing. Both brands have International Yacht Racing Union recognition and maintain high quality standards.

In open class racing, anything goes (within open class design regulations). The racer is free to design his own board or to modify a brand name board. A word of caution to the new open class racer. There are a number of freesail products available today that would not qualify as high performance crafts and are difficult to use in over 15 mile per hour winds. Choose your board carefully keeping speed in mind. Dennis Davidson, the first freestyle champion in North America, says, "The level of competition in Hawaii and Europe is so tight that it becomes important to have good equipment. The point is not to stagnate yourself with equipment that is not fulfilling your needs." To this end, a small group of freesailors in Hawaii is quietly working away making innovative adjustments to the hull, sail and booms. In time these new developments will improve the craft and the sport.

This is not to say that brand name boards cannot be raced in open class competition. They can be with modifications to the hull, sail, daggerboard and uphaul. Any brand name board is, of course, perfectly suited to recreational freesailing and the recommendations below apply to the purchase of a new brand name board as well as a high performance board.

A high performance freesail craft is often a hybrid board made by combining components from different sources. For some freesailors a full custom board constructed of exotic synthetics is the only answer to their quest for speed and performance.

Hull In open class racing the weight of the board and the rig are very important. Generally, the lighter the board, the faster the freesailor will go. Look for something in the 22 to 33 pound (10 to 15 kilogram) range. If possible try to weigh the hull and all the existing components when they are dry.

Some freesailors prefer larger
sail windows for increased
visibility, particularly when
sailing downwind.

...sail equipment should be
...able so that it can be used
...rowded beaches like this

The hull should be very flat in the aft to the middle section with a pronounced rise in the bow. The sag of the hull is another important factor to consider. Freesailors differ in opinion as to the amount of sag that is necessary. Some say a board should be supple because it rides the waves better than a hard board. Others say a supple, soft board is prone to material fatigue. Basically, it becomes a matter of personal preference, where you are sailing, and how long you want the product to last.

Daggerboard and Skegs   Twin skegs are essential to stability at high speed but are not necessary in light winds. Consequently, a hull providing for multi-skeg setups is desirable. The daggerboard should be adjustable (moveable aft or forward) so that it will be efficient on all points of sail. See that the daggerboard has the proper shape and fits the daggerboard area snugly.

Mast Assembly   The mast base must be able to pivot so that the rig can be free-mounted with nylon or stainless steel components. It should be covered with a soft material to minimize sharp edges and cuts to the feet.

The mast should be stiff and strong. Graphite fiber and aluminum masts meet these requirements; however, they are expensive. A stiff mast is better suited to beating in high winds. A flexible mast reacts better in squalls and gusts, because it will give under pressure and neutralize some of the wind's force. Glass fiber masts are standard on many boards and are functional for most applications.

Sail   A well-cut sail, when it is rigged on the mast and booms, should flex the mast to the point where it becomes rigid. A tight leech and foot makes the rig rigid and not apt to change shape radically under heavy wind loads. Look for 3.8 ounce dacron for long-life sails.

Booms   For open class and one design racing, the competitive freesailor should have aluminum booms. Look for booms with a rubberized grip and strong urethane or nylon fixtures that are screwed or riveted to the boom ends. The front end piece should form a tight link between mast and booms. This piece is very important because it is difficult to achieve a snug connection without it. The booms should also have cleats that allow for adjustments to be made while sailing. For racers, it should be noted that the less flex in the booms, the more precise the trimming. Flex can be tested by applying force between the port and starboard halves of the wishbone.

Uphaul   An elastic uphaul (or bungied uphaul) should remain tight between the booms and mast base. Fixed to the mast base, it should always be there when it is needed, never flailing out of reach. The uphaul should be one-quarter inch (.6 centimetre) prestretched braided dacron line.

Antislip Feature   A rule of thumb to follow here is: the less slippery the boat, the better the board. However, be wary of a surface that is too hard, because the chance of abrasion is high. The deck side of the hull should have fittings for footstraps to prevent slippage in advanced freesailing.

Used Boards

In any purchase, price is always a factor and a second-hand board may be the answer for some freesailors. A top brand freesail craft loses about ten per cent of its value annually, whereas a cheaper brand can lose as much as seventy-five per cent. To ensure that you are getting top quality for your dollar, the purchase of a used board should be done through a dealer. Generally, look for a moulded plastic hull, aluminum booms and, if you are small in stature, a small rather than a full-sized sail.

Hull   Look the hull over for cracks and tears. Tears allow water to be absorbed by the foam core. A good indication of water retention is the weight of the board. Lift the board up and see if it weighs more than you think it should. Compare it to other boards in the store or check the specifications for new boards.

Run your hands over the upper and under surfaces of the hull to check for soft or spongy areas. If at all possible, stay away from fiberglass boards as fiberglass is very brittle and shatters easily.

Beware of tape on the board—it is probably hiding a defect. Weak points are covered up and loose screws are strengthened with tape.

Daggerboard and Skeg   The daggerboard is a good indication of the care given the boat by the previous owner. If it is damaged you can assume that the boat has been run aground.

Look for tears in the daggerboard well. If there are cracks, you cannot be sure how much water has seeped into the foam filling. Again, if possible, weigh the board.

Take a skeg key or screwdriver along with you when purchasing a freesail craft. Unscrew the skeg and check that there are no cracks or holes in the fixture groove.

Mast Assembly   Watch for tape around the bottom of the mast and remove it to check for splits in the fiberglass material. Damage is most common in the bottom of the mast and the part of the mast where the boom is attached. Look these areas over carefully for any signs of wear and tear.

If the mast foot is wooden, make sure that the screws are in place and that the wood has not split. Also, check the universal joint for sand and see that it rotates freely.

Rhonda Smith, a top
competitor , uses one
design class equipmen

il cloth should be
rable and made out of
ounce dacron.

Booms Immerse aluminum booms, if possible, to see if they are taking in water. Cracked, split or damaged material in the booms is a good indication that the boom may be absorbing water. Check the inhaul and outhaul cleats to make sure they are secure and not worn out. If the booms are wooden check for splits in the laminations.

Boards for Ocean Freesailing

Most of the boats on the market today are designed for lake sailing. The ocean sailor will need a craft developed for ocean sailing. Because of the larger waves on the ocean, a freesail hull must have a more upturned nose to keep it from diving between swells. Few boards are designed this way but polyethylene/foam hulls can be modified through heat treatment, giving exactly the amount of "scoop" required for your particular sailing application.

Footstraps are the number two requirement for ocean sailing. They serve as bindings to keep the feet attached to the board in the white water of breaking waves and make wave jumping possible. Again there are few boards marketed with footstraps, but if you are a do-it-yourselfer, substantial savings can be had by building a custom craft and adding your own footstraps. Although it does not look professional, footstraps can be glued to most hulls with epoxy resin.

Maintenance of Equipment

Freesail equipment is easy to maintain. After sailing on the ocean, or a lake for that matter, you should remove all sand from the universal joint, the hull and the sail. This will increase the length of time your equipment will last.

Any cracks that appear in the hull should be repaired immediately to prevent water from being absorbed by the foam core. You can fix cracks yourself using a hot-melt (thermoplastic) glue gun and all-purpose glue sticks. If you aren't adept at repair work, it is best to approach a dealer about repairs.

Teak wooden booms should be teak oiled about two or three times a season and before putting the board away for the winter. If boom delamination occurs, stop it by pouring epoxy resin or glue into the affected area. Ocean sailors should remove salt from aluminum booms to prevent corrosion.

Keep your sail out of the sun for long periods because ultraviolet light will make the sail brittle. Dry the sail before placing it in a sail bag and be sure to take the battens out before folding and storing your sail. When your boat is rigged but not in use, slacken the downhaul and outhaul lines.

Storage of the board is simple. Place it on its edge on a flat dry surface.

CHAPTER 12
Freesail Apparel

Safety is the major factor to consider when purchasing this part of your freesail equipment. Since the freesail craft is an extremely wet boat, care must be taken to guarantee adequate warmth and buoyancy capabilities in your freesailing wear.

Mike Gadd and Carol Tayl wear full wetsuits.

Wetsuits

An essential accessory for extending the freesail season beyond the warm summer months and a way to make those windy, cold summer days more pleasurable is the wetsuit. The combination of wind and water can cause a loss of body heat, which in turn can cause a loss of energy. This may lead to intense coldness and possibly hypothermia (see Appendix 1). A wetsuit will help prevent this problem.

The wetsuit provides a layer of insulation between the body and the suit. This minimizes heat loss from the body. Neoprene, a synthetic rubber filled with tiny air or nitrogen bubbles, is the most commonly used material for wetsuits. It is very elastic and, although it is not an approved life jacket, it provides a certain amount of buoyancy.

Pure neoprene provides the best type of insulation, but it is not durable enough to use alone in a suit. A synthetic lining, such as nylon or lycra, is essential on the inside for added strength. Suits that are lined on both sides are more durable, but do not insulate as well as suits that are lined on one side. The reason for this is that an external synthetic lining absorbs water while the shiny black neoprene lets it run off. Heat loss through evaporation is therefore much higher for the double-lined suits. Suits with a rough textured neoprene on the outside are not as warm as those with a smooth neoprene because the water does not run off as easily.

Both types of wetsuits are usually warm enough in cool weather conditions. If you do not plan to sail in cold temperatures, the choice between the two types is an esthetic one. Suits that are lined on two sides can be many different colors whereas neoprene on one side has only one color—black. Combinations with double lining on specific parts of the suit are also available.

The thickness of the neoprene suit depends on the severity of the conditions. The neoprene wetsuits were originally designed for divers. The freesail suit does not have to be as thick as a diving suit because the freesailor spends more time out of the water than in the water. An eighth-of-an-inch (.32 centimetre) thickness is recommended because it does not inhibit the mobility required in freesailing.

The wetsuit creates a thin layer of water between the neoprene and the body. The thinner the layer of water, the better. A tight fit is therefore mandatory. The fit should be snug around the groin and shoulder areas but movement in the armpits and knees should be maximized. Be sure to check for abrasive seams.

A number of freesail wetsuits have been adapted from the diving world. Unfortunately, many provide for only specific climatic conditions. The jacket with beaver tail, trousers, shorty (with and without sleeves), the overall, long johns and bolero top all have limited use. For example, the overall suit leaves you with the decision of all or nothing on moderately cold days. Most jackets

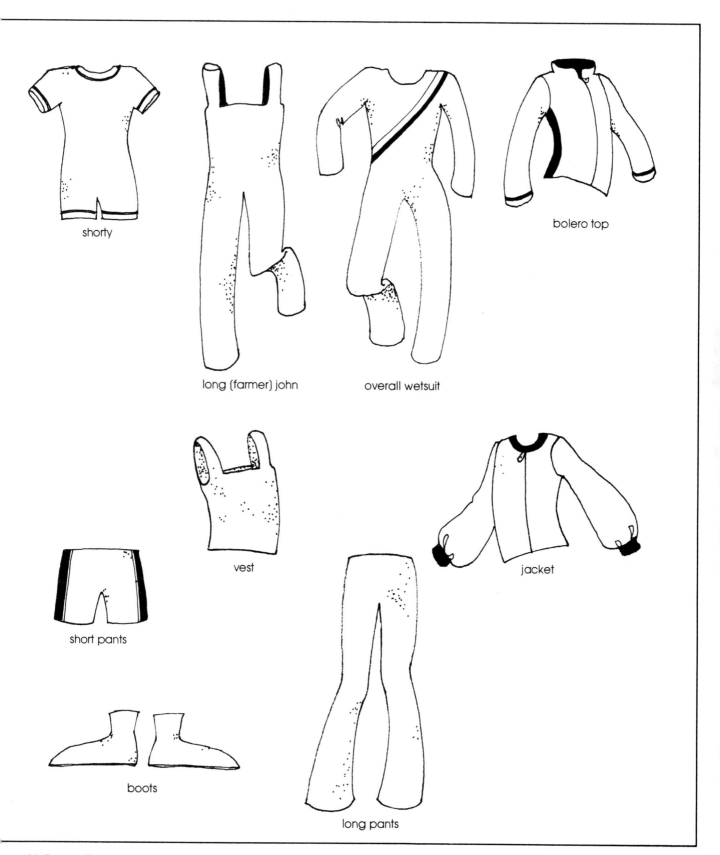

shorty

long (farmer) john

overall wetsuit

bolero top

vest

short pants

boots

long pants

jacket

Figure 11. Freesailing apparel

seem to confine the wrists and arms causing very quick fatigue and most pant legs fill with water from the bottom in higher winds. The farmer john is the most useful suit and can be worn with a simple windbreaker on moderately cold days and a bolero top on very cold days.

We suggest that you build a wetsuit wardrobe that allows you to go out in virtually all weather conditions. A wardrobe should consist of boots, short pants, long pants, vest (no arms), and a neoprene jacket with long arms made of lined wind-resistant material and with neoprene cuffs. The pants should have a slight flare at the bottom to prevent water accumulation in higher winds. The jacket should have arms which are loose and wind resistant. The torso and sleeves should be made of neoprene. This flexible system equips you for freesailing in southern climes (vest only) and in late fall to winter conditions in the north.

A wetsuit is expensive but with good care should last a long time. Rinse it in fresh water after ocean sailing and keep it out of the sun. Don't let it freeze in the winter. A wetsuit will add months of pleasure to your freesailing season. Choose wisely and maintain it properly.

Other Equipment

There is other equipment available to the freesailor which will make the sport more pleasurable.

If you find your feet get cold on cool days, you could invest in a pair of neoprene boots. They generally cost between $40 to $50. Running shoes will do if you don't want to buy boots, however, they obviously won't be as warm.

A windjacket under the farmer john wetsuit helps to keep the arms and back of the neck warm. The best ones resemble ski shells and are sold by most freesailing dealers.

On long sails, gloves can prevent calluses and blisters. Specially designed gloves for freesailing are on the market; however, some freesailors use golfing gloves or gloves that gymnasts use. These can be purchased at most sporting goods stores.

To avoid sunstroke, it is always a good idea to wear a visor. Visors with freesailing logos on them are available from most dealers.

In some areas you are required by law to wear a life jacket. The kind you buy should be comfortable and government approved. A tested, government approved jacket will keep the head above water, increasing survival time in cold water.

Running shoes can be worn to keep the feet warm.

To avoid sunstroke it is a good
idea to wear a visor.

Appendices

Hypothermia

Hypothermia is much more than feeling a chill. It is a killer. If a freesailor does not know how to cope with this particular condition, death is not unlikely.

Hypothermia occurs when intense cold attacks the major core areas of the body such as the heart and brain. Clinically, heat is lost within the body at a faster rate than it can be regenerated by burning food and fat reserves.

An individual in the state of hypothermia will undergo a number of physical and mental changes. In extremely cold water the body reacts to protect itself. Shivering is one sign of hypothermia. The body shivers as a means of creating heat to stop the fall of the core body temperature. Blood supply to the extremities is reduced and body metabolism is increased through a higher breathing rate and heart beat. These reactions occur because the body is trying to protect the heart and the brain from heat loss.

Hands and feet lose heat at a high rate because of their cylindrical shape. The high heat loss in these areas causes a reduction in manual dexterity, touch discrimination and movement in the muscles and joints.

Cold water quickly drains an individual's strength and swimming one hundred yards or climbing out of the water becomes almost impossible. Mentally, there is an overriding sensation of pain. According to Joseph McInnis in **The icy facts on how cold water kills**, "Anxiety and confusion are mixed with a feeling of impending doom, particularly if help is not an arm's length away. Judgement, memory and reason are impaired and within minutes the individual is teetering on the abyss of panic."

The survival time in cold water depends upon the weight of the individual (heavier people have more fat that can be regenerated into heat), the temperature of the water and the person's physical capabilities.

Survival time is increased if the sailor gets out of the water by climbing on top of the hull. Heat loss in the air is less than heat loss in the water.

There are two main areas of the body that suffer high heat loss: the sides of the chest and the groin region. To prevent heat loss in these areas, hold the inner sides of the arms tightly against the chest and press the thighs together and raise them to close off the groin area.

If you see someone suffering from hypothermia, check for a doctor in the area and call an ambulance to move the person to a hospital.

To rewarm a victim of hypothermia, huddle people together around the victim. Place hot wet towels, water bottles, electric and chemical heating pads or heated blankets on the individual. Hot, non-alcoholic drinks and a hot bath or shower may also help. Be sure that you don't rub the surface of the victim's body or jolt him in any way.

Before you go out freesailing, check the weather and water temperature carefully. During cold water and weather conditions wear a neoprene wetsuit to prevent rapid heat loss. Also make sure that there is a retrieval boat close at hand so that if you do get into trouble on the water there is someone to pick you up. Most of all use common sense.

APPENDIX TWO
Freesailing on Ice and Snow

Iceboating is the sailor's winter alternative. This option is also open to the freesailor who can hook his sail to a tri-runnered platform and sail at 40 knots over the ice. On snow, hulls made of polyethylene (the same material is used in ski bases) will move much more quickly than on water, approaching 30 knots of speed.

A word of caution. There obviously is risk involved in careening across a hard medium while standing up and trying to hang onto a runaway sail. Helmets and hockey or football equipment are recommended to provide adequate body protection.

As the craft begins to move in even the lightest of winds, the friction between the runners and the ice is so minimal that the craft accelerates instantly to five times windspeed. Apparent wind plays a very important role in sail control when such speeds are attained.

There are a number of freesail icecraft commercially available in Europe. Most are made to accommodate standard aquatic freesail rigs with peg—or tee—type mast bases. Some rigs can be screwed on. However, the design is quite elementary, and a comparable apparatus can be built for very little money. Simply cut a 5 ft. 9 in. (1.75 m) long, 3 ft. (1 m) wide triangle of thick plywood and add angle iron runners at each corner, sharpening the rear two for a good grip on the ice to keep the craft from slipping sideways. The dull-edged front runners allow the bow of the craft to be pushed laterally by the legs. The sharp rear runners assume the function and position of a daggerboard on a water hull.

As mentioned above, polyethylene hulls will slide over the snow, but not as quickly as hulls equipped with runners will slide over ice. A much shortened skeg will prevent the stern from skidding out, but without a means to establish lateral resistance, the boat will not sail well upwind. A fun day of fast reaching will prompt most aficionados to devise an icecraft more suited to speed and performance.

Freesailing on ice should be done in a large open area of clear ice, free of snow patches and any obstacles, moving or stationary. These craft are not as manoeuverable as aquatic hulls and require much more room to tack, jibe and come to a stop, in part because of the higher speeds involved. Don't go off chasing snowmobiles and iceboats until you've had an opportunity to practise the basic skills!

Northern sailors whose lakes freeze, but don't receive much snow cover, are in an ideal situation to expand their fleet activities into the winter months. Patchy or solid snow-covered ice will inhibit performance, but with a hybrid snow—ice boat on very shallow runners, good performance can be expected in less than ideal conditions.

This aspect of the sport has a future with advanced freesailors. High wind experience is necessary to handle the higher windspeeds involved. Beginning freesailors should only try ice sailing with very small sails to keep the speed down. And don't forget the helmets and pads. Ice is hard stuff!

Glossary

Aft   Toward the stern of the craft.

Amidships   Toward the middle of the craft.

Apparent wind   A change in wind direction caused by the forward speed of the boat.

Astern   Behind the stern.

Backwinding   Occurs when the craft is going faster than the true wind causing the opposite side of the sail to fill with air.

Beam reach   A course 90° from the wind.

Bear off   To change course away from the wind.

Beat   Sail upwind. Also the upwind leg of a race.

Bow   The most forward part of the hull.

Broad reach   A course aft of 90° from the wind.

Clear (or clean) air   Wind that is not affected by other boats or obstructions.

Cleat   A small plastic device to which a line is tied. Securing a line on a cleat.

Clew   The lower corner of the sail which is farthest from the mast.

Close hauled   Sailing as close to the wind as possible.

Close reach   A course forward of 90° from the wind.

Dirty air   Wind that has been affected by other boats or obstructions.

Downwind   Away from the direction from which the wind is blowing.

Fore   Toward the bow of the craft.

Head off   See bear off.

Head to wind   On a course that is heading directly into the wind.

Head up   To change course toward the wind.

Heading   A point on the horizon to sail towards.

Hull drag   Frictional resistance on the hull caused by the movement of the hull through the water.

Jibe   To bring the boat around onto a new course by turning the hull downwind and around onto the new course.

Knot   One nautical mile (6060.2 feet) per hour.

Lateral resistance   The hull slides to leeward while sailing. This is counter-acted by the size and shape of the daggerboard.

Leech   The edge of the sail between the head and the clew.

Leeward   Away from the wind. The downwind side of anything.

Luff   A sail will luff or flap loosely when it is not completely full of wind.

Mark   A marker or buoy that boats sail around in a race.

Offshore wind   Blowing away from the shoreline.

Onshore wind   Blowing from the water to the land.

Pinch   To sail too close to the wind, preventing the boat from making progress upwind.

Point   To sail close hauled.

Port   The left side of a boat when viewed from the stern.

Port tack   When the wind is filling the left side of the sail and the left hand is closest to the mast, the craft is said to be on a port tack.

Railing up   The hull flips up onto its side or rail.

Rake   To lean the sail to port, starboard, fore or aft.

Reach   A course across the wind. See beam reach, broad reach and close reach.

Running with (or before) the wind   Sailing with the wind blowing directly behind the craft.

Sheet in   To fill the sail with more air by pulling the sail in with the aft hand.

Sheet out   To dump wind from the sail by easing the sail out with the aft hand.

Spill wind   See sheet out.

Starboard   The right side of a boat when viewed from the stern.

Starboard tack   When the wind is filling the right side of the sail and the right hand is closest to the mast, the craft is said to be on a starboard tack.

Stern   The aftermost end of the hull.

Tack   Being on a tack is sailing a

constant course. Tacking in freesailing is bringing the boat around onto a new course by turning the hull up into the wind, stepping around the front of the mast to the opposite side of the sail and bearing off onto the new course.

Trimming the sail   Sheeting in or out to obtain maximum power from the wind. Fine tuning the sail.

True wind   The wind that is felt on a craft that is not moving. See apparent wind.

Upwind   Towards the direction from which the wind is blowing.

Weather, to   See upwind.

Wind shift   A change in the direction of the wind.

Windward   Towards the wind. The upwind side of anything.

3956

Acknowledgments

Derek Debono 13, 78, 99 (right)

Steve Hill 2, 4, 6, 8, 11, 14, 15, 19, 20, 22, 26-37, 47, 64 (left), 65, 70, 72, 77, 88, 93, 98 (above right), 100, 102, 104, 105, 108, 109, 111, 112, 116, 117

Tim Jacobs 83

Sara Lee 57, 68, 69, 81, 96, 98 (below left and right), 99 (above left)

Bill Petro 113

Dana Richardson 53, 82 (above and left)

Ron Rimer 60 (left)

Chris Speedie 52, 56

Steve Wilkings 60 (above), 61, 64 (below), 86, 87, 90, 91, 94, 95, 97

Windsurfing International Canada 12, 74